ON SHIFTING SANDSHOES

Surviving The Great Australian Holiday
An 'in tents' experience

Written by Paul Davies
Directed by Mark Shirrefs
Production Manager Susan Weiss
Designer/Drawings/Slides Amanda Johnson
First Performed at TheatreWorks, December 1988
Produced by Far Out East Productions,
Mullumbimby Civic Centre July 2009
(directed by Richard Vinnycomb)

This book is copyright. Apart from any fair dealing for the purpose of private study, research or review, as permitted under the Copyright Act, no part may be reproduced by any process without written permission. Inquiries concerning publication, performance translation or recording rights should be addressed to the author

Any performance or public reading of *XXXXXXXXXXXXX* requires a license from the author. The purchase of this book in no way gives the purchaser the right to perform the play in public, whether by means of a staged production or a reading.

© The moral right of the author has been asserted.

Bringing the World
Back Together

A Picture Play

NORTH STRADBROKE ISLAND
(MINJERRIBA)

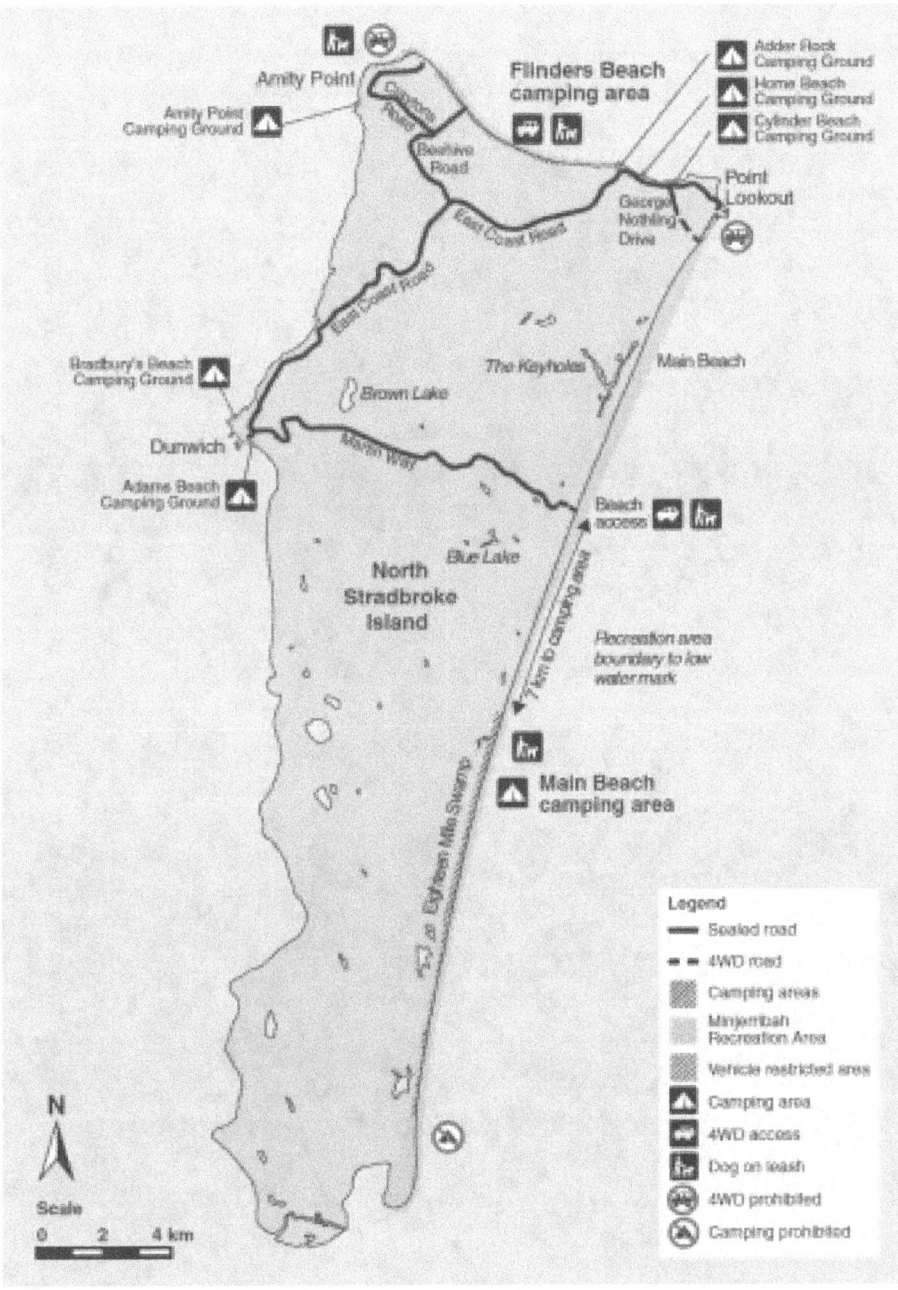

CONTENTS

Author Note		6
Cast and Crew (1988)		7
Characters		9
On Shifting Sandshoes (text and pictures)	ACT I	13
	ACT II	109
Original Camp (1983/84)		169
Critical Reception		173
2009 Production		193
Author		195
Dedication		197

AUTHOR NOTE

Photo © Ruth Maddison

The human experience in Australia has been sited overwhelmingly in some kind of temporary camp. From the gunyahs of the aboriginies to the tents of the First Fleet and the goldfields, Australians have housed themselves impermanently. And even now, despite our weatherboards and brick veneers we still answer, every summer, some primitive urge to escape from "civilization" and camp under the stars. The characters and events portrayed here are entirely fictitious and bear absolutely no resemblance to a camp held on Flinders Beach on Stradbroke Island in 1984 from Boxing Day to New Year's Eve. The play was written in close collaboration with Mark Shirrefs and the cast. Their wonderful comic talents and elegant wit are smudged on the final draft forever…

ORIGINAL CAST and CREW (1988) :

Photo © Ruth Maddison

L-R: Paul Davies (author), Rosie Tonkin (Paula), Jean Kittson (Diane), Caz Howard (Margot), Dave Swann (Raoul), Ross Williams (Bruce), Brian Nankervis (Sandy) Mark Shirrefs (director)

PRODUCTION CAST (1988) :

Jean Kittson (Diane)
Kris Keogh (Margot)
Rosie Tonkin (Paula)

Bryan Nankervis (Sandy)
David Swann (Raoul)
Ross Williams (Bruce)

CHARACTERS

BRUCE McKENZIE. Is a Gold Coast property developer who has weathered several boom/bust cycles and managed to ruin only a small number of peoples' lives in the process. Bruce loves being the centre of attention, plays jokes on people, enjoys his prosperity (when not technically bankrupt), is pretty unscrupulous at everything he takes on, bows to no authority (especially moral ones) and likes his footy, his car, his dog, his bank manager, and his wife in that order.

MARGOT McKENZIE. Bruce's long suffering wife, managers a beauty parlour in Indooroopilly called "Curl Up And Dye" which Bruce basically funded to give her something to do. Obsessed with appearances, Margot fancies herself as something of a 'designer' with a certain BrizVegas flair. A perfect match for Bruce in many ways, Margot nevertheless finds an outlet for her 'artistic' side in the companionship of Raoul Manon. Who she defers to in all things and even supports financially when the charming chef finds himself 'between engagements' - as sadly, he so often tends to be, on account of his inherent shyness about working terribly hard.

RAOUL MANON. Is always charming and amusing. Loves taunting Bruce, has found a reliable friend in Margot and puts up with her because she laughs at all his jokes and always helps him out. His natural charisma is best expressed through his ukelele playing. It always manages to work an audience over.

DIANE ALLSOP. Athletic, articulate, and single- again. Diane is a teacher and tends to be a bit bossy, especially with men, who she finds generally never quite grow up out of the Grade 8/9 phase.

PAULA O'BRIEN. Shy, quietly talented. Self effacing. Paula dreams of becoming a professional singer but hasn't really cracked it yet. Sandy's her new boyfriend and after an awkward six months getting to know him she's finally brought him up to the annual camping holiday to meet her old Brisbane gang- especially Diane and Margot who she went to teachers college with all those years ago.

SANDY MILLS. Inner city Melbourne born and bred and someone who's rarely been outside a 10 km circle that includes Fitzroy/Carlton and Prahran/St.Kilda. Sandy fears raw nature in places such as Stradbroke Island because of the number of discomforts to be endured there and the many threatening species of wildlife (including insects). Virtually every item of clothing Sandy owns is Black. Including his Trotskyite Cap and Dunlop Volley sandshoes.

FLINDERS BEACH
(MINJERRIBA)

ON SHIFTING SANDSHOES

ACT ONE

It's December 1988, it's Queensland, and it's a remote campsite on Flinders Beach, North Stradbroke Island (Minjerriba). The island lies in Moreton Bay about thirty kilometres off the coast from Brisbane. Travel there is by vehicular ferry only.

The Straddie Barge

1. ARRIVALS CAMPSITE   (XMAS EVE)
BRUCE, MARGOT

Sunrise on Christmas Eve. Lights come up on a tent which has been pitched in the centre of the stage with a folding chair and cooking gear spread neatly around it nearby.

Into this pleasant scene staggers BRUCE, pushing a purloined shopping trolley loaded with several slabs of beer and an esky.

>BRUCE. (turning back to urge her on) Margot! Hurry up, we'll be late...

On spotting the tent however, BRUCE collapses onto the sand exhausted. He's appalled by the sight of the tent.

BRUCE. Oh kerrist ! Look at this ! Can you believe it!

MARGOT, with their tent, boogie board, and two suitcases full of clothes staggers up behind him.

>BRUCE. If you hadn't spent so much time packing we'd have made the first barge.

>MARGOT. I'm on holidays, Bruce. I'm not going to be bossed around by you.

>BRUCE. Why bring so much stuff to Straddie when all you do when you get over here is take it all off again !

>MARGOT. Don't have a heart attack, Bruce. We can just go further up the track till we find another clearing.

>BRUCE. But this is *our* camping site. We pioneered this spot. We've been coming here every Christmas for *seven* years. I planted those banksias.

MARGOT. We don't own the place, you know. If it belongs to anybody it belongs to the traditional owners. We should take a moment and acknowledge we are standing on Noonuckle land.

BRUCE. Margot, this is Queensland. Okay?

He moves towards the tent, chucking the folding chair, towels, surf toys and cooking gear etc. inside.

MARGOT. What are you doing!?

BRUCE. Survival, of the meanest. Margot, that's our' motto. Beautiful one day, greedy the next.

MARGOT. Bruce, you're tampering with some person's private property!

BRUCE. Look- this is close to the road, it's got plenty of shade; protected from the wind, fifty metres from the surf... it's perfect.

He finishes gathering all the gear inside the tent.

BRUCE. Besides, the others are all heading here, it's the only place
they know.

MARGOT. Can't we just leave a sign saying: "Raoul, George, Di,
Craig, Paula and friend gone further up 'the track' keep walking...?

BRUCE. Who do you think we are, Burke and Wills ?

MARGOT. We can't just move these people.

BRUCE. Why not ?

Margot has to think about it.

MARGOT. They might be bikies or something.

BRUCE. One clump of tea trees is just the same as any other to some of
these brain dead morons. I mean. Look at this tent...they must've only bought it yesterday.

BRUCE has undone the support ropes all round the tent and is now floundering about inside.

BRUCE. Will you come and grab the other side please! Do something useful with your life.

MARGOT. BRUCE, I'm hot, my head is thumping from that ridiculous footy club party you dragged me to, and all I intend to do today is open my banana lounge and slip quietly into it with a Bourbon and Berocca.

BRUCE. (re-emerging through the tent flap) Do you want them to spring us doing it ?!

Margot sighs, drops her gear and reluctantly scrambles into the tent with BRUCE...

2. ENTER DIANE
BRUCE, MARGOT, DIANE, PAULA, SANDY

... just as DIANE arrives from her early morning jog along the beach.

She pauses to do some stretches and catch her breath and then stares, incredulous as the tent appears to walk off by itself.

DIANE. Freeze !

Inside, BRUCE and MARGOT freeze.

>BRUCE. (inside tent) Eh !?

>MARGOT (inside tent) Oh god ! Bruce ! (gulp)

>DIANE. Stop or I'll hit you with a frying pan! (grabbing it from the fire
>place)

>BRUCE. (inside tent) What !?

DIANE whacks the outline of BRUCE's head through the tent. There's a hollow, ringing sound.

BRUCE GROANS and collapses inside, pulling the tent down with him.

At which point PAULA and SANDY arrive, also loaded down with gear.

>PAULA. Diane !

>MARGOT. (inside tent, pleading) Don't kill us !

DIANE (urgently to PAULA and SANDY) There's burglars in my tent.

PAULA. (turning to her man) Sandy, don't just stand there, do something.

SANDY. (nervous) Do something ?

PAULA. Yes- stop them !

SANDY. What- now ?

PAULA. No, next week ! (pushes him forward)

Trying to summon some courage, SANDY drops his load and throws himself at the outline of MARGOT inside the tent, wrestling her to the ground.

MARGOT SCREAMS.

SANDY. (proudly) Got him.

MARGOT. (still inside tent) Do something, Bruce.

BRUCE GROANS.

DIANE. (recognising the voice) Bruce?

MARGOT. (inside tent) Diane?

PAULA. Margot?

DIANE. Margot?

MARGOT. (inside the tent) Paula!

BRUCE. Diane!

PAULA. Bruce!

BRUCE also manages to disentangle himself and crawl out one end of DIANE'S now totally wrecked tent, rubbing his head. DIANE points the frying pan at him aggressively.

>BRUCE. (laughs, relieved) Don't shoot, don't shoot, we surrender.

>DIANE. (annoyed)Where the hell were you anyway? I waited at the first barge till quarter past and just managed to get the last
>car space on board.

>BRUCE. Margot couldn't find her eyeshadow.

SANDY helps disengage MARGOT from the tangle of ropes as she also emerges from the wreckage. As soon as she's free MARGOT whacks BRUCE with a flipper from DIANE'S stash of surf toys.

>MARGOT. You're like a bull in a china shop.

>BRUCE. At least we haven't lost the site.

>DIANE. (indicating her tent) You broke it you can fix it Bruce.

As BRUCE sets about grumpily restoring DIANE'S tent ... MARGOT suddenly throws her arms wide.

>MARGOT. Paula !

>PAULA. Margot !

DIANE comes over to join in the three way hug.

PAULA. Di !

DIANE (hugging PAULA) I miss you, kiddo. Melbourne's too far away.

Sandy stands back, feeling a little out of his depth. BRUCE continues restoring DIANE'S tent.

3. CATCHING UP
BRUCE, MARGOT, DIANE, PAULA, SANDY

MARGOT. You look good, though Paula.

DIANE. Fantastic. Still too pale. Must be that southern winter. I suppose all the beaches are too cold...

PAULA. Well yes, it's not really a (beach culture)...

MARGOT. (riding over her) Last year you looked like a worn out dish cloth.

PAULA. (laughs) No- I didn't.

DIANE. You did, Paula, you had big bags under your eyes. (shaking the under parts of her arms) To go with your floppy bats wings.

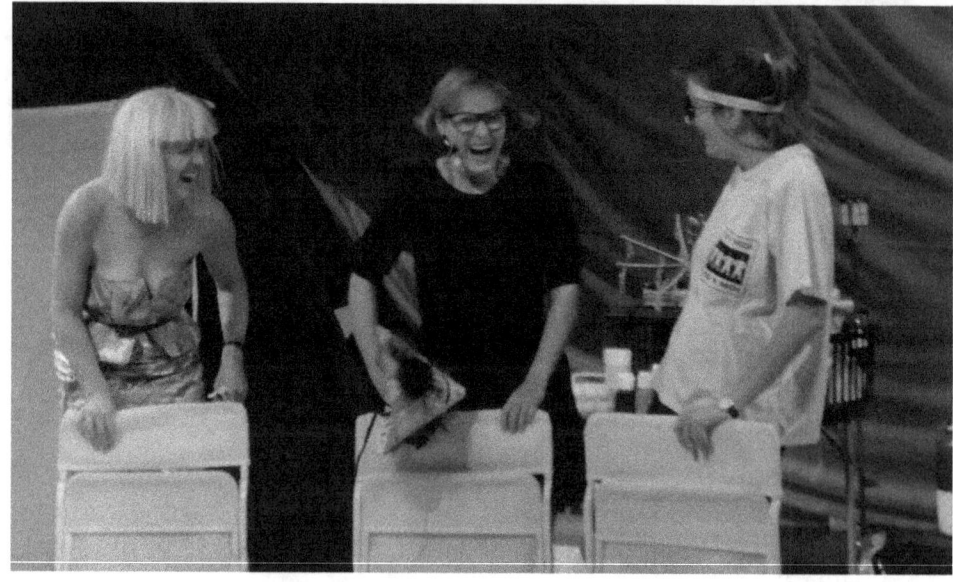

PAULA. Stop it ! (laughing) Diane ! You're terrible. Cruel. It's the headmistress (coming out).

DIANE. What about the band? (to Margot) Did you hear about Paula's band, Margot ?

MARGOT. (all ears) What?

DIANE. Go on tell her.

PAULA. Oh it's no big deal, really.

DIANE. You know how Paula's always had this fantastic voice- well now she's in an all women's band.

MARGOT. Oh no.

PAULA (shy, coy, modest) We're just writing some songs at the moment, see how we go. Taking it one step at a time.

DIANE. What are you called.

PAULA. The *Twisted Sisters.*

MARGOT. There's no money in it, though.

DIANE. Margot ! You always put money at the top of everything.

MARGOT. No I don't.

DIANE. There is money isn't there Paula ? You always see rock stars at glamourous parties holding onto some young model or a rising soapie star...

MARGOT. You'll have to bring the girls to my salon. We'll create a look.

PAULA. (uncertain.) A look? We're sort of traditional, really.

DIANE. What ? Folk songs? Country and Western?

PAULA. No- more Joanie Mitchell. Kind of thoughtful ... More into, you know, being who we are...

PAULA breaks into SONG : a few bars from the A side of the *Twisted Sisters* proposed single ...then back to

PAULA. So ... developing- well, developing "a look" is not what we're about- it's more to do with the music. And the words.

MARGOT looks somewhat underwhelmed.

> MARGOT. Well anyway, let me host a party for your next Brisbane tour. I'll invite all the A list. People in radio, that sort of thing. People from the Coast. Noosa...

> PAULA. Yes, well I'm not sure when that will be. So...

She sort of trails off, so there's a pretty awkward pause. PAULA still seems
hopeless. MARGOT has nothing to say. BRUCE continues setting up the camp: putting out chairs, pitching tents, unloading gear.

> PAULA (searching for another subject, turning to MARGOT) So...You've got a salon now?

> MARGOT. Bruce helped out with the lease. I have to admit. But he's doing very well at the moment. In fact we're expecting a big contract to be signed next week. I forget how many units...

PAULA. What's it called?

MARGOT. (misunderstanding) I can't say- it's all very hush hush. Government contracts, private public and all that…

PAULA. No- I meant the salon...

MARGOT. Oh. "Curl Up And Dye".

DIANE. You'll love the colours, Paula.

MARGOT. We got Sue Benson to do it. (still thrilled) She finally said 'yes'!

PAULA. Who?

MARGOT. I forgot- you're a southerner now. She's one of Brisbane's top interior people.

DIANE. She does sheets too, and mugs and pillow cases.

MARGOT. We were desperately lucky to get her. She rarely takes on small jobs. But … look at you, (standing back from PAULA spelling it out) you look fabulous.

DIANE. The bloom of love. That's what it is.

PAULA. (shyly) No...

MARGOT. No, it suits you, Paula. You look entirely different in the face- Lost all the puppy fat.

DIANE. (turning to SANDY) I'm guessing he must be the reason why...

DIANE and MARGOT turn to look at SANDY. He's still hovering the background feeling a bit out of place. PAULA disengages, turns from the two women, and moves over to include him.

PAULA. Sorry- Margot, Di, this is Sandy Mills.

SANDY nods shyly. They ad lib "hullos" SANDY and PAULA shake.

MARGOT. You're younger than Paula are you Sandy ?

PAULA. (warning) Margot !

DIANE. He looks younger than you, Paula.

SANDY feels like a shag on a rock.

MARGOT. How old are you, Sandy?

SANDY. I'm not very good with figures.

DIANE. I thought you ran a bookshop?

SANDY. Anyway, time is river. We all age in our different ways.

PAULA. Oh stop it, both of you. (squeezing SANDY'S hand)

DIANE. We've heard all about you, Sandy.

SANDY.(shy smile) Nothing bad, 1 hope.

The women LAUGH.

4. BRUCE MEETS SANDY
BRUCE, SANDY, PAULA

Finished with setting up camp, BRUCE blusters over, holding his palm out and downwards. Putting SANDY in the submissive posture.

BRUCE. G'day, mate, Bruce McKenzie.

SANDY. (uncertain) Er- g'day...

BRUCE. Manager for Queensland.

SANDY. Oh... Manager for … what...exactly

BRUCE. Depends what you want ? (LAUGHS)

PAULA. Bruce is a sort of property developer.

SANDY. (not sure what to think) Oh- really. . .

BRUCE. (proudly) One who made the Gold Coast what it is today.

SANDY. Oh, right, gee that sounds impressive, unfortunately I've never been there.

BRUCE. (disbelief) What?

> PAULA. (leaping in) Sandy's hardly ever left Carlton.

> SANDY. I want to St. Kilda once. My first big trek to the beach.

The others look totally nonplussed. Is he taking the piss? Or what?

5. THE KOMBI SAGA
BRUCE, MARGOT, DIANE, PAULA, SANDY

They all set about pitching their tents (which all get erected over the next couple of scenes).

Since DIANE'S is already up, she starts on the kitchen/dining area (setting up a folding table under a fly with a hammock of groceries stretching across).

MARGOT, retreats to her banana lounge, to work on her tan, helping herself to an early morning glass of bubbly.

> DIANE. (noticing it) Is that a herpes, Sandy?

> SANDY (alarmed, feeling his lip) What?

> MARGOT. I hope you're not kissing him, Paula, not while it's at the infectious stage.

> PAULA. It's not herpes. It's a cut from the crash.

> DIANE. Crash?

> PAULA. We pranged the Kombi near West Wyalong.

> SANDY. (still annoyed by what happened) We?

> PAULA. Sorry- I, I pranged Sandy's Kombi when a freak wind blew our trailer into an oncoming semi.

> MARGOT. (shock) Oh, no! Paula, are you alright?

PAULA. (nods) Bit shaken.

SANDY. The Kombi's a write off.

PAULA. Yes, alright, Sandy, I'm sorry about Lulu.

BRUCE. Come on you two, no domestics allowed except on the Bastard Ball court.

BRUCE picks up and punches a basket ball at SANDY

BRUCE. Get your sandshoes on, it's Queenslanders versus the Mexicans.

SANDY. (to Paula) What about the car...

MARGOT and DIANE start improvising a volley ball net

BRUCE. It's too late to worry about that over here Sandy, you're on Straddle to enjoy yourself.

PAULA. He means the other car.

BRUCE. (confused) Eh?

PAULA. We used the hundred and fifty we got for the Kombi to hire a Falcon.

SANDY. Which she promptly bogged half a mile back.

PAULA. You weren't game to drive through sand, remember, Sandy.

BRUCE. You didn't try and drive in over the creek !

SANDY. But it's still miles away- we had all this gear.

MARGOT. No one drives in over the creek, Sandy.

BRUCE. This is a protected area, mate, the whole of Straddle's just one big pile of sand. The only thing holding it together is the vegetation.

MARGOT. That's why we always park back on the bitumen and walk in.

SANDY. There weren't any signs...

DIANE. Have you seen the damage a four wheel drive can do to the frontal dune system

SANDY. It was only a Falcon.

BRUCE. That means you're probably stuck there.

SANDY. Oh great.

PAULA. Sorry, I should've remembered.

BRUCE. (punching a basket ball at him again) A quick game of Bastard Ball'll soon get the trip out of your system. Come on Di, you're playing for Queensland now.

SANDY. But the car …

MARGOT. You don't own it.

BRUCE. And no one's going to steal it are they ?

They all LAUGH.

6. PITCHING TENTS
BRUCE, MARGOT, DIANE, PAULA, SANDY

BRUCE starts hitting the ball across the net to SANDY who fumbles it awkwardly.

PAULA is having trouble erecting their tiny two-man pup tent.

32

PAULA. (pleading/demanding) Sandy, will you help me with this, please ?

SANDY. (But)...I've never put a tent up in my life.

PAULA. Come on, where are the pegs ?

SANDY. Pegs - What for a washing line?

PAULA. Tent pegs, you said you packed them.

SANDY. No I didn't.

PAULA. I saw you put them in the box with the sleeping bags.

SANDY. Well that was on the . . .

SANDY & PAULA Roof-rack !

PAULA. Oh no, I never even thought to check for it.

SANDY. It certainly wasn't on Lulu when I buried her.

PAULA. Alright ! I'm sorry about the Kombi alright !

SANDY. I won't say another word (about it.)

Paula and Sandy try to spread out the tent again, Sandy gets it all fumbled up.

PAULA. (gives up) Look, why don't you just go and get another load from the car.

SANDY. I can't.

PAULA. Why not !?

SANDY. (searching his pockets) I think I've locked the keys in the boot.

PAULA. Oh Sandy !

DIANE. I've got some spare pegs... (bringing them over) Boomerang brand.

PAULA. Thanks, Di, I'll make sure you get them back .

DIANE. I can't believe you've never put a tent up, Sandy.

SANDY. I've seen pictures of them in books.

PAULA. Sandy's father never enrolled him in the boy scouts.

DIANE. Pity. I can just imagine you in little khaki shorts with a toggle round your neck.

The women LAUGH.

SANDY. What, you think that's funny? Pity your father never enrolled in driving lessons, Paula- sorry- sorry, won't say another ... (to Diane)
She's a great driver, just doesn't notice semi-trailers coming.

PAULA. I couldn't help it Sandy, even the cops admitted that.

DIANE. Oh Kombi's are notoriously unstable, very high centre of gravity.

SANDY. What's that smell ?

He sniffs the end of the tent he's still holding.

SANDY (CONT'D) Smell that Paula.

PAULA. It's just been treated, it's only waterproofing that's all.

SANDY. I might be allergic to it.

MARGOT. Have you got many allergies, Sandy ?

SANDY. Five that I know about.

He's inspecting the label on their tent.

> SANDY Has this stuff got nylon in it ?
>
> PAULA. (losing patience) Just grab the other end, alright ?
>
> SANDY. You know I break out in a rash.
>
> PAULA. We came up here to forget that sort of thing.
>
> SANDY. The inventor of nylon committed suicide, did you know that ?

By now PAULA has the basic shape of their tent up- without much help from SANDY.

> SANDY. Is that it ?
>
> PAULA. (presenting it) Da Dah!
>
> SANDY. It looks so tiny.

Sandy goes inside.

> SANDY. Paula I can't possibly sleep in here, I can't even stand up. I'll get claustrophobia.
>
> DIANE. Are there any phobia's you haven't got Sandy ?
>
> SANDY. Oh look here's a little window.

He pokes his head brightly through the tent window just as:

7. ENTER RAOUL
BRUCE, MARGOT, DIANE, PAULA, SANDY, RAOUL

Raoul grooves in on his rusty bicycle, playing "Stayin' Alive" on his ghetto blaster.

The WOMEN go wild, ad lib EXCITED GREETINGS.

>MARGOT, DIANE, PAULA. Raoul ! Darling !! At last...Now the party begins.

Hugs and air kisses between RAOUL and DIANE, MARGOT and PAULA.

>RAOUL. (embracing them blowing air kisses) Careful of the suntan cream.

>MARGOT. Looking good, Raoul

>RAOUL. Feeling good, darling. Feeling...(sexily) dangereux.

LAUGHTER and more big sloppy kissing embracing between RAOUL and the WOMEN. He's obviously popular.

>MARGOT. Drink.

>RAOUL. Just a fizzy mineral, Margot, I'm dieting this morning.

>DIANE. You don't need to, you look gorgeous Raoul.

Raoul takes the compliment modestly. As his due.

> RAOUL. Keep talking. I'm listening.

More amusement from the girls ... As MARGOT fetches him his drink-with ice.

Again SANDY'S left on the outer... just as BRUCE emerges from his and MARGOT'S tent, having finally got it all sorted out inside.

> BRUCE. Raoul !

BRUCE and RAOUL size each other up like gunfighters, then go into their ritual Maori Haka. (A leftover from their rugby their playing days at University).

Sandy emerges from his tent, spots the war dance and goes straight back inside.

> RAOUL & BRUCE. (slapping thighs and elbows, poking out their tongues) Hunga Hunga Yugga Ma, Hoo Hoo Blah de Blah, Animal Animal Ya Boss Ka !

PAULA. (explaining to Sandy) Raoul and Bruce went to Queensland Uni together.

SANDY looks less than impressed. Paula brings him forward practically dragging him into the circle...

PAULA. Raoul Manon - Sandy Mills.

SANDY is terrified that he's going to have to do the Hunga Hunga routine as well.

RAOUL. (holding out his hand) G'day, mate.

SANDY. Pleased to meet you, Raoul.

RAOUL. You've got great hands.

SANDY would like to pull away, can't just yet.

PAULA. Raoul runs La Mediteranné restaurant in the Valley.

RAOUL. You must come sometime, be my guest.

SANDY. (making sure to include Paula) We'd love to.

RAOUL unloads a small back pack and a set of dumbells from his bike.

BRUCE. Hang, on, hang on where's the meat ?

RAOUL. (slight distaste) Meat !? (already with the glass of bubbly in his hands)

BRUCE. That was the arrangement, Raoul. Margot and I bring the wine and beer Di brings fruit and vegies, Paula brings the breakfast stuff and *you* bring the meat.

PAULA. Actually, I've got to apologise about the breakfast stuff.

SANDY. The box was smashed in the Kombi… (quickly) sorry, sorry, won't say another…

RAOUL. Okay, Okay, I've brought some wild rice and a tofu pie. Alright? (be grateful)

BRUCE. (appalled) Tofu!!

RAOUL. That's all I could manage on the bike. It was high tide...

BRUCE. You managed your frigging Dumbells !

RAOUL. (throws his hands up) You see ! Meat makes you aggressive. That's why I've become a vegetarian.

BRUCE. Hitler was a vegetarian.

RAOUL. Hitler was a Capricorn.

MARGOT & PAULINE & DIANE. He was not!

RAOUL. (nudging SANDY) Spot the Capricorns.

DIANE. Actually he was an Aries.

But BRUCE'S mind is on only one thing.

BRUCE. Ferkerrisake! There's at least seven of us now, staying for a *whole week*. We need *steak*, we need *chops* and *sausages*. *Mince*, *camp roasts*, whole *chickens*, *ham*, *bacon*...And all he's brought is his bloody weights! I can't believe it!

MARGOT. Raoul can cycle into Dunwich on Monday and stock up at the butcher shop.

BRUCE. No, no, I have to go back to Brisbane on Monday- just for the day- to conclude a very big deal, I'll stop at the butchers on the way back.

RAOUL. Don't martyr yourself, Bruce, that halo might fall down and choke you.

PAULA. Can't George pick up something when he comes over ?

AWKWARD SILENCE. RAOUL looks down. And collapses into one of the folding chairs with a deep SIGH.

DIANE. George isn't coming.

BRUCE. What ?

MARGOT. We don't talk about George anymore.

BRUCE. Why not ?

SANDY. Who's George ?

PAULA. (for Sandy's benefit) Raoul's...friend.

RAOUL. It's alright. It's just a minor hick up.

MARGOT. Minor! Raoul's on the phone to me the other day- in tears- for hours.

DIANE. I thought we said we weren't going to talk about it.

BRUCE. (increasing frustration) Talk about what ?

DIANE. Look, let's leave it there shall we

Pause. But BRUCE can't help himself.

BRUCE. What happened to George, Raoul?

MARGOT. I warned you, Raoul. I told you there was something sneaky about him. I never liked George from the start.

BRUCE. What did he do !?

MARGOT. George ripped off Raoul's stereo and hocked it for some dope.

BRUCE laughs. MARGOT stands behind RAOUL and starts massaging neck and shoulders- offering sympathy.

DIANE. (censoring) Margot!

PAULA. Must've been a bit of a shock, mate.

RAOUL. (groaning pleasurably) Just a little bit lower Margot, you know my tension spot. (back to Paula) Bit of a shock! I was in love with the bastard.

MARGOT rubs the back of his neck. RAOUL moans pleasurably.

> BRUCE. Oh we're all *bastards* here. And you know what bastards play?
>
> BRUCE, DIANE, PAULA (gleefully) Bastard Ball !!!

8. BASTARD BALL
BRUCE, MARGOT, DIANE, PAULA, SANDY, RAOUL

They LAUGH and square off on the volley ball court. Which DIANE has rigged up beside the kitchen area. SANDY isn't too sure about what exactly is going on. MARGOT remains horizontal on her banana lounge.

> BRUCE. Come on, Margot, you're playing for Queensland too.
>
> MARGOT. Bruce, I'm having a glass of bubbly and I'm cheering Raoul up.

> BRUCE. Raoul, you're a whimp you can play with the Victorians.

Seething, RAOUL picks up a cricket bat and moves menacingly towards BRUCE with it.

MARGOT. (fearful) Raoul!

But instead of braining BRUCE. Raoul spins the bat in his hand.

RAOUL. Your call shithead.

RAOUL spins the bat up into the air...

BRUCE. In memory of George - "humps."

The bat drops and RAOUL lunges at BRUCE grabbing him by the collar of his haiwaiian shirt. Angry! Finally!

RAOUL. (screaming) Just shuddup about George !

There's a moment where RAOUL might be about to do some serious damage to BRUCE. Dangereux indeed. But the tension passes and subsides, BRUCE is smiling, not really worried.

BRUCE. Spin the bat bugalugs and brace yourself for a thrashing.

RAOUL. Flat side.

RAOUL spins the bat and depending how it lands.

BRUCE (OR) RAOUL. Best of three.

DIANE grabs the basket ball and cuts the men short.

DIANE. Come on we'll be here all bloody day.

BRUCE. That's the whole point, Di. We have got all day. That's why we're here.

And so BRUCE, MARGOT and DIANE square off against SANDY, PAULA
and RAOUL. MARGOT is a player but still holds her drink.

DIANE. We'll serve.

RAOUL. Straddie Rules.

PAULA. Just don't hit a tree, Sandy.

DIANE punches the basket ball over the net and instead of punching it back SANDY just catches it.

SANDY. What... !?

PAULA and RAOUL. Replay ! Replay !

So DIANE serves again and SANDY hits it over towards the trees.

BRUCE. (gleefully) Hit a tree ! Hit a tree !

BRUCE MARGOT DI (pointing at them) Bastards! Bastards! Bastards!

RAOUL and PAULA start talking at once, vigorously protesting.

RAOUL. That wasn't a tree, that was a shrub.

PAULA. The sun was in his eyes. He doesn't know the rules.

RAOUL. We weren't ready.

PAULA. Di wasn't behind the line.

DIANE. 'Course I was...

MARGOT. Someone moved the thong.

PAULA. Margot touched the net.

RAOUL. That corner doesn't count.

BRUCE. (victoriously waving his arms from side to side) Queens-land Queens-land.

DIANE. Come on, Bastards, Bastards. (insisting on the rules)

So, reluctantly PAULA and RAOUL start hopping around on one leg, calling out:

PAULA RAOUL. Ark Ark Ark Ark Ark.

MARGOT. Come on Sandy, you're in it too.

And so SANDY starts hopping and calling out

SANDY. Ark ark Ark Ark Ark....

BRUCE. Go the mighty maroons! Go! Go! Go !

SANDY. (under his breath) Morons...

But luckily nobody seems to hear it. DIANE serves again and the Victorians are now forced to play the point hopping around on one leg...calling out "Ark Ark Ark" until this time … Margot hits it out on the full.

RAOUL, PAULA (immediately) Bastards. Bastards…

So now BRUCE, DIANE and MARGOT have to hop on one leg, causing MARGOT to spill her drink.

BRUCE, DIANE, MARGOT. Ark Ark Ark Ark Ark

As PAULA goes to serve. . .

BRUCE. Shit Margot, will you put that stupid drink down and take this seriously. You're almost as bad an alky as George was.

RAOUL breaks off playing and furious once more moves under the net straight towards BRUCE, ready to thump him.

RAOUL. I'll bloody kill him !

DIANE and PAULA have to separate the men. RAOUL has his fingers round BRUCE's throat who keeps LAUGHING, not taking any of this seriously. Until finally:

Margot frumps off in a huff.

MARGOT. You're like a child sometimes.

BRUCE. God! Now where are you going?

MARGOT. I'm going to change.

And she goes inside their tent to put on one of her elaborate beach ensembles.

BRUCE. We've got to have even sides, Margot.

48

    She just ignores him.

In the gap of silence we hear a strange GROWLING NOISE.

9. BLINKY
BRUCE, MARGOT, DIANE, PAULA, SANDY, RAOUL

    SANDY. (curious, mild alarm) Hang on, what's that sound ?

    PAULA. What darling?

    SANDY. Like a horse vomiting.

    BRUCE. Raoul always cries like that.

    DIANE. That's not Raoul- that's BLINKY !

    PAULA. Yes, there he is- there's Blinky !

The game breaks up. . .as they all "OOH" and "AAH" over the koala sitting on the branch of a nearby gum tree.

    PAULA Isn't he gorgeous ?

BRUCE. (all coy and soppy) Aw…Blinky ! Look, Margot, Blinky's here.

No response from the tent. BRUCE persists with his soft and mushy act.

BRUCE. Look, Margot- you're favourite little baby bear's turned up.

It brings her out- in a dazzling one piece with matching coat and hat.

MARGOT. Hullo, Blinky Winky, it's Margot Mumsey Wumsey.

SANDY. What's a Blinky ?

PAULA. Can't you see the Koala ?

SANDY strains to look up, a bit short sighted. All that reading…

SANDY. Oh, right, "Blinky Bill", right, how, ah...how obvious. (seriously starting to wonder what he's doing here)

BRUCE. Sort of a camp mascot, really. Little beggar turns up every year.

PAULA. Aah, Blinky ! You know we always come back don't you?

DIANE. (explaining to SANDY) Actually, Blinky's a very rare Blue Koala. There's only a dozen of them left in the wild. Most of them on Straddie

SANDY. Only dozen! Should we give him some Gogii berries or something? Rescue Remedy? Ginseng ? Kale?

DIANE. (smirks at his ignorance) They don't drink Ginseng, Sandy. They don't even drink water. In fact Koala's only eat gum leaves.

PAULA. That's why they look so stoned all day.

> BRUCE. (prodding him again, pushing it) Look, Raoul, Blinky's back.

> RAOUL. (storming off) I couldn't give a *stuff* about Blinky.

BRUCE wants to keep playing.

> BRUCE. Come on Sandy, get your sandshoes moving.

Throwing the ball at him again

> BRUCE (CONT'D)
> It's not over yet.

> SANDY. (protesting) I thought this was supposed to be a holiday.

> DIANE. It *is* a holiday. What else are they for?

> SANDY. Playing games?

> DIANE. You really are from Melbourne aren't you?

She turns back to RAOUL who's slumped in a chair again. Starts massaging his neck.

> DIANE. Where does it hurt?

> RAOUL. (melodramatic) Mostly in my soul.

SANDY GROANS (audibly). PAULA stabs a warning look at him.

> RAOUL. But if you could concentrate on the superspinatus, Di...just there, oh...yes...(groan of pleasure) Oh, Di- that's soooo good...(desperate) Will you marry me.

She LAUGHS.

>DIANE. You sound like one of my grade elevens.

>RAOUL. Lucky them.

All of which leaves only BRUCE and PAULA left playing on the Bastard Ball court. The ball hits the net and drops under it into the centre of the court.

They come together over the ball, both reaching to pick it up off the ground...where they pause and hold each other's look - for just a fraction too long.

Eventually PAULA turns away, a little flushed. Hoping SANDY didn't notice. BRUCE follows her exit.

10. MORNING TEA
BRUCE, MARGOT, DIANE, PAULA, SANDY, RAOUL

It's the cue for BRUCE to start opening cans from his huge pile of slabs of beer.

>BRUCE. Ok, that's it, bugger it- if that's the general attitude. Morning Tea everyone!

BRUCE reaches into his large esky and pulls out a handful of stubbies.

>BRUCE. (handing him one) Morning tea, Sandy.

> SANDY. Oh, ah, actually, I only drink pinot noir, thanks. And never before lunch.

> BRUCE. (uncomprehending) What ?

BRUCE regards SANDY as if he's from another planet. And a pretty alien one at that.

> SANDY. The yeast in beer reacts with my colon. I get terrible wind.

DIANE can't resist a GUFFAW. He's weird alright.

> BRUCE. (shaking his head/what a dingbat) Geezus.

BRUCE moves on to sneak up behind RAOUL as DIANE continues to work his neck and shoulders.

BRUCE. Morning Tea, Raoul.

BRUCE drops the cold stubbie on RAOUL'S relaxed torso. Propelling him forward out of his chair in shock.

RAOUL. Ah!!

But RAOUL takes it, nevertheless. Pissed off. BRUCE chuckles.

RAOUL. (cursing BRUCE) Nature killer. Capitalist pig.

BRUCE just laughs off the insults. And RAOUL takes his beer to set himself up in the hammock with a book.

PAULA, SANDY, MARGOT and DIANE are gathering around the folding table and chairs that DIANE has set up under the fly in the centre of the camp which now has it's three tents (DIANE's neat, practical dome, MARGOT & BRUCE's large pretentious one, and SANDY and PAULA'S tiny pup tent)

DIANE. Hands up those who'd like a nice cup of camonmile?

SANDY. I'd kill for a double strength soy laté.

DIANE. Good, the wood's over there, off you go. You can pretend to be a hunter gatherer, Sandy. (still amused by him)

She hands him the axe, SANDY looks like he's never held one before.

SANDY. (half reminding himself) The sharp bit, right?

But he's joking of course. And disappears towards the wood pile. The sound of frenzied chopping and a lot of GRUNTING NOISES from Sandy are heard off as DIANE and PAULA start carving up the first Xmas cake.

DIANE. Where's your tent Raoul ?

RAOUL. Tents ! How bougeois.

PAULA. Tell me that when it starts to rain.

RAOUL. But you miss out on the stars inside a tent. Where's your sense of glamour ?

MARGOT. (slight concern)You're not serious? What- you've only brought a sleeping bag?

RAOUL. Sleeping bags are for whimps. All I want to do tonight is lie across a dune and feel the whole weight of the planet heaving beneath me.

BRUCE. That's the soldier crabs mate, scrambling to get out of the hole you've blocked off.

BRUCE laughs, happy to be getting RAOUL back, he unscrews his own stubbie, takes a sip.

BRUCE. Ah- I wouldn't be dead for quids: a stubbie in one hand...

RAOUL. Your manhood in the other, moving up and down vigorously...

BRUCE (ignoring that, running on)...a warm sun beating down...a classic surf calling...

RAOUL. (low) Wanker.

BRUCE. Raoul sulking in the background... Ah Queensland... Perfect one day, even more brilliant the next.

MARGOT. (raising her glass) Let's live a little.

The rest join her in the toast as SANDY re-enters with the axe and one tiny piece of tea tree.

All together:

    PAULA. To life!

    BRUCE. Cheers!

    DIANE. Skoll!

    RAOUL. Campai!

    MARGOT. Salut!

    SANDY. Yeah, right.

Not having a drink yet, SANDY just hangs there with the tiny branch he's managed to cut. Then decides to try and make a fire...as the rest hoe into Xmas cake and various drinks.

11. CUT OFF
PAULA, MARGOT, SANDY, DIANE, BRUCE, RAOUL

>PAULA. Don't you love the idea that we're actually cut off from the mainland? I mean the very idea of an island, it's so primitive... So real...
>
>MARGOT. (agreeing) 30k from a city of a over a million people and we could be light years away from any concept of civilisation.
>
>SANDY.(glad to interrupt his fire making) Civilization ! Brisbane ! (mocking) Brisneyland!!! the *Cold* Coast. Surface Paradox. Don't make me laugh…

He laughs. Finally feeling superior.

The Queenslanders (everyone else- including Paula) are not amused. They just stare at him.

>BRUCE. (feeling betrayed) I thought you said you hadn't been there.
>
>MARGOT. (pleading) We had Expo. We had the Commonwealth
>Games.
>
>DIANE. Weren't they marvellous? I took my Grade 8s to Expo seven times.
>
>BRUCE. They said we'd never do it. (shaking his head) But we showed the world. Showed them what Progress is all about.
>
>SANDY. Progress !? What? To bulldoze what little history you've got left!

BRUCE. (getting serious) Well, you see, we're more concerned with the future than the past up here, Sandy.

PAULA. But you don't have a future until you acknowledge the past.

BRUCE. Oh here we go … the bloody Mexican attack...you're just jealous of our weather. Our lifestyle...

DIANE. (to PAULA) You're talking to a property developer don't forget.

BRUCE. (defensive) One who's about to make quite a substantial contribution to the overall amenity of the place.

DIANE. For which you'll receive an inordinate amount of public money.

BRUCE. I take the risks. I'm out there travelling on the seat of my pants sometimes- just to make a bit of difference. To make things better. We build places/shops/parks and gardens that other people come and live in and get to enjoy for a very long time.

RAOUL. Funny thinking of you as a developer, Bruce, you're probably the least developed human being I know.

BRUCE. Oh thank you very much, Raoul. What is it, get stuck into Bruce week? All I've done for you: Revamping La Mediteranné's kitchen, putting that verandah on your crumbling shack in West End.

SANDY. When Melbourne was the capital of Australia this country had the highest standard of living in the world.

DIANE. But we're not in Australia now, Sandy, we're on Minjerriba.

SANDY. Minjerriba? Is that an aboriginal term?

MARGOT. That's the original name for Stradbroke Island. It was/is Noonunkle country.

BRUCE. I thought it was the name of a wine cooler.

MARGOT Oh Bruce ! You really are too much sometimes.

BRUCE. I think we could get a DreamWorld thing happening over here and call it "Mingerribaland" I can see it now: dolphin pools and witchetygrub burgers. . .

DIANE. (hits him) Bruce! You're disgusting. (slight pause) Why am I surprised?

MARGOT. (passing it round) Speaking of food, more Xmas cake
anyone- Paula, Di ?

DIANE. (holding a hand up) Thanks Margot, I've had my quota of saturated fats for the day.

SANDY. Saturated fats ? Should I give them up too ?

BRUCE. Oh don't start her off forgodsake !

SANDY can't find a seat, sits on an esky.

DIANE. Pritikin reckons you can make it to 120 if you eliminate the bad fats: red meat and dairy products.

BRUCE. All you're creating, Di, is a beautiful corpse.

SANDY. I wish I could give up something. My life is a series of addictions: Proust, Pinot Noir, extremely good coffee, barracking for Collingwood.

BRUCE. Collingwood! What a loser. I rest my case.

DIANE (keen to encourage him and ignore BRUCE)
You *can* do it, Sandy. Anyone can. Even Bruce. You can change your whole life in a moment and never look back.

BRUCE. Why am I surrounded by people who
always want to look back!

DIANE. Put that beer down now, Bruce. Make "no more alcohol" your New Year's resolution and you'll avoid the heart attack that's surely coming.

BRUCE. Di, I've finally decided that your health kick is more boring than Margot's travel stories.

He jumps up and grabs the basket ball.

BRUCE. Come on Sandy, Raoul, second set, meat eaters against the vegos, we'll soon see soon who's fit...

DIANE. Enough ball games... Time for a surf.

PAULA. (checking the time) God! Nearly mid day- it's almost too
late.

SANDY. Is the sun dangerous now?

MARGOT. Depends what you're wearing, Sandy.

MARGOT takes off her beach coat to reveal her new beach outfit. It has the desired effect.

RAOUL. Wow Margot.

MARGOT. (coy, seeking/hoping for his approval) Do you like it?

RAOUL. Go, Margot!

MARGOT. Thank you Raoul.

He's earned his brownie points for the day.

12. AT THE BEACH
BRUCE, MARGOT, DIANE, PAULA, SANDY, RAOUL

As a group they grab towels and head for the beach.

So that BRUCE, outnumbered and left holding the ball, is forced to give up on another set. He throws the Bastard Ball into the food hammock, grabs the beach umbrella, Margot's banana lounge, a few more stubbies, and follows the rest of them to the beach...

As they emerge from the relative shade of the campsite onto open beach the sun seems even brighter.

SANDY is rugged up against it (umbrella hat, zinc cream etc,)

SANDY. I can't see any flags. Where are the lifesavers ?

RAOUL. Relax, man, no one's been taken by a shark over here in weeks.

SANDY. Sharks !

RAOUL. This is Straddie, mate, not St. Kilda beach.

MARGOT. It's wild, it's primitive.

DIANE. What's the matter, Sandy, don't you like the sun?

SANDY. There's no way I'd be exposing myself at this time of the day.

PAULA. Sandy doesn't get much sun in Melbourne.

SANDY. We're more a night culture.

DIANE. Are you afraid of getting skin cancer Sandy?

SANDY. You know there's a hole in the ozone layer now the size of Antarctica.

MARGOT puts on an extraordinary looking bathing cap.

MARGOT. Do you think this might help?

It wouldn't but it's quite colourful.

PAULA. That's an amazing hat, Margot.

MARGOT. I'm predicting the bathing cap will make a big comeback. I've still got my mother's collection from the fifties.

BRUCE. Mightn't keep the sun off but is certain to frighten the sharks away. Stick with her, Sandy.

MARGOT. (showing it off) Do you like it?

PAULA. Yes.

DIANE. No, not much.

MARGOT. (slight hurt) I picked it up in Paris last year, I think it's a bit of a giggle.

PAULA. I didn't know you'd gone overseas, again.

MARGOT. My dear, I've just come back from Europe transformed !

BRUCE. My bank account's been pretty transformed by it too.

PAULA. I've heard Paris is very expensive.

MARGOT. Darling, they even charge you to go to the toilet.

BRUCE. That wasn't a toilet, Margot, that was the "Loo-v-re"

An old joke, but BRUCE loves it. SANDY rolls his eyes. Behind them RAOUL remains absorbed in his novel in the hammock.

MARGOT. You've got to see it though- in the flesh. It's tremendously exciting. I think once Bruce passes on I could live in Europe.

BRUCE. Who'd want to live in freezing bloody gay Paree when you've got a glorious beach like this on your back doorstep! (slight pause)
Anyway, Margot you might go before me.

MARGOT. What a horrible thought.

DIANE. Not the way you're drinking.

BRUCE. Just think of that. You might cark it first and I might have to spend what remains of our little nest egg on some meter maids down at Jupiters.

MARGOT. Yes, you'd squander it all if I wasn't around to control your urges. (to the others) He still hasn't done anything about the visa card.

DIANE. What?

MARGOT. I had my visa card stolen in the Vatican.

PAULA. Oh no.

DIANE. Why didn't you report it?

BRUCE. Cause the bloke who took it's spending less than Margot !

SANDY can stand it no longer and braces himself before heading off to the surf still wearing his t-shirt and sun protection gear..

BRUCE. Don't forget your water wings, Sandy. (sharp turn back to:) Raoul !

BRUCE throws a frisbee at RAOUL who catches it and throws it back.

SANDY. (waves) If I wave like that- it means I'm drowning.

RAOUL. (doing wierd hip and arm gyrations) And if he waves like this it means he's lost his togs.

They LAUGH, SANDY disappears. BRUCE and RAOUL chase the frisbee off towards the water, flinging it between them.

13. GIRL TALK BEACH
MARGOT, DIANE, PAULA

This leaves the women alone to shake out their towels and start working on the tan.

Eventually when they take up their possies, working on the front first.

>PAULA. (shaking her head at BRUCE's exit) He's so manic about sports. Where does he get his energy from? No offence Margot, but Bruce doesn't look all that fit does he? Stacking on the kilos.
>
>DIANE. Bruce has got to get on top of people before they get on top of him. Missionary position McKenzie. A classic case.
>
>MARGOT. Oh he looks all giddyied up and full of energy now but come 2pm he'll be flat on his back in the tent snoring.
>
>DIANE. I think he's terribly insecure...The constant joking...It's all a front. Has he ever had any affairs, Margot?

PAULA suddenly looks uncomfortable.

>DIANE. That you know about?

>PAULA. (distracting from the topic) Oh, is that a dolphin! No, it's Sandy. (she waves) Yoo Whoo ! (excited) He's caught a wave!

>MARGOT. I don't know I never ask.

>DIANE. (to Paula) How are you and Sandy getting along ?

>PAULA. (too quickly) Fine !

>MARGOT. Doesn't look like it.

>PAULA. We had a rough trip that's all.

>MARGOT. You've hardly stopped bickering since you got here.

DIANE. They weren't bickering, Margot.

MARGOT. A six month old relationship! They should still be in the after glow of all that early lust.

DIANE. When the object of your desire can do no wrong.

MARGOT. And things that later drive you insane are still cute little foibles.

PAULA. Sandy just isn't a very public person. He doesn't display his emotions like that.

MARGOT. For the first year and a half Bruce and I could hardly keep our paws off each other. He was my wild jungle man and I was his raven haired queen.

PAULA. Raven?

MARGOT. Yes I changed colour that year, just for a couple of weeks.

DIANE. I remember that year- it was embarrassing in the tents at night. You were so loud, Margot.

PAULA. We all had to turn up the radio and pretend we couldn't hear anything.

PAULA and DIANE start making moaning/groaning sounds- mimicking MARGOT'S audible love tryst with BRUCE.

MARGOT. (laughing, embarrassed) Oh don't- I wasn't.

PAULA. You were. You always had a high sex drive, Margot.

DIANE. She sounded like she was being strangled.

More MOCK EROTIC GROANING sounds from the two woman chorus.

DIANE. (laughing) I had to stop Steve from going over to rescue you.

Slight pause.

PAULA. Wasn't that Alan ? That year?

DIANE. (slight embarrassment) Oh- 81, yes, Alan. How could I forget.

MARGOT PAULA DIANE (distastefully) Alan !

They LAUGH. It's cut short by SANDY'S re-entry. SCREAMING.

> SANDY. Aahh! Aahh! Paula ! Paaaula ! (breathless panic) A box jelly fish!! Kerrist.
>
> PAULA. (real concern) Sandy !
>
> SANDY. (exposing his pale arm a full of red welts) Look. Right across the forearm. I'm gone, Paula.

He displays his wound, wet and shaking.

> DIANE. (examining it) Relax Sandy, it's only a bluebottle.
>
> SANDY. Relax ! I may only have seconds to live.
>
> PAULA. (going to get it) It's alright Poppet, there should be some vinegar in the hammock.
>
> DIANE MARGOT (not impressed) Poppet?
>
> SANDY. It hurts, Paula.
>
> PAULA. I know, darling, I know, just hang in there I'll be right back.
>
> MARGOT. Actually just- try this.

She starts rubbing the contents of her glass on it.

> SANDY. Bourbon! Aaah ! (it stings like buggery)
>
> MARGOT. It'll take the sting out.
>
> SANDY. Ow! Ow ! Not according to my first aid manual.

PAULA comes back and helps him back into his sun protection gear. He lies moaning quietly, holding his arm under the shade of the umbrella.

RAOUL comes back in from the surf.

> RAOUL. Fantastic body surf. Big thumping dumpers that make you feel like you're being chucked out of a two storey building.
>
> SANDY. It was awful, like a nightmare.
>
> RAOUL. No, it's great. It's like ... wrestling with God.

BRUCE comes in from his swim.

> BRUCE. Who's he tagging with these days, Hulk Hogan?
>
> DIANE. Sounds like we might have to crack a few, Paula? (you coming?)
>
> MARGOT. I'll just dabble at the edge.

As the three women move off.

> SANDY. Paula ! My skin condition- I think it's reacted with the salt water ... Paula!

But she's out of earshot. Effectively leaving the three men alone, BRUCE is bouncing a tennis ball on his cricket bat.

14. BOY TALK   THE BEACH
BRUCE, SANDY, RAOUL

SANDY is trying to change out of his wet togs, he's wrapped his beach towel around his waist but it keeps slipping down.

> BRUCE. Come on Sandy, French cricket you're bowling.

BRUCE hits the tennis ball at him while he's still on one leg with the togs. It tips him off balance. RAOUL and BRUCE LAUGH .

> SANDY. (at the end of his tether, almost in tears) Bruce, I'm exhausted, I've lost a car, been in an accident, got hopelessly bogged, I'm hot, I'm itchy, the sand is giving me a rash ... Can't you just give it a rest for a goddamn minute!

RAOUL. What's the matter with you, man ? You seem so uptight. Relax brother.

SANDY. Have you ever come face to face with death ?

RAOUL and BRUCE exchange a look. What's he on about now?

SANDY. If you thought - in a week's time you might not exist- what would that mean?

Slight pause.

BRUCE. Do you want to bat then ? (offering it to him)

SANDY. (utter frustration) God! You people! You just haven't got any idea have you. Of what it would mean to not be here ?

RAOUL. What's the hell difference does it make? Enjoy the sunshine, man, take your clothes off, get a really good tan.

SANDY. All you think about is your body.

RAOUL. Yeah, could you rub some lotion on it for me ?

> SANDY. Haven't you ever thought about what it means to be *alive*? Truely alive! I mean where were you BRUCE, before you were here?

> RAOUL. He was with me, we were at the pub getting pissed. Relax, mate, you're far too tense.

Raoul starts rubbing Sandy's shoulders.

> SANDY. (jerks away, awkward) Look, I don't want to relax. Okay. Thank you but no.

> RAOUL. You're not homophobic are you?

> SANDY. Certainly not. Definitely. No.

> RAOUL. Well then- relax...

RAOUL starts massaging SANDY again and now SANDY has to contain his natural instinct to pull away.

> BRUCE. Do you want to play frisbee then?

SANDY. Look. I *do* want to relax- but my idea of relaxation is like- look at the ocean.

They look. Think a moment.

BRUCE. It's big, it's there, it's wet.

SANDY. (relaxing under Raoul's massage) It's so blue today.

RAOUL. Yeah, that's amazing because sometimes it looks like- blue and then later in the day it looks sort of. . .

SANDY. Green ?

BRUCE. (weighing his hands) Greeny-Grayish. Sort of smokey green.

RAOUL. Yeah, I dunno- maybe it is a visual thing.

SANDY. It's like the sky. The sky can be blue.

BRUCE. But very rarely green.

SANDY. And the trees, the trees are always so...

BRUCE. High ?

RAOUL. Unless they're young trees.

SANDY. And the sand- it's so white.

Another pause for wonder.

SANDY. I wonder if snow's ever fallen on this beach. Can you image that ? Close your eyes and imagine that ?

SANDY closes his eyes, RAOUL and BRUCE share a look, nod back towards the camp bar, mime having another drink and silently creep away- unbeknown to SANDY who keeps his eyes closed, deep in meditation.

15. WOMEN ON MEN   THE BEACH
MARGOT, DIANE, PAULA, SANDY

SANDY'S still deep in meditation as the women return from their swim.

> SANDY. I wonder if the ocean ever froze over- whether you could step from the sand onto ice?

The girls share a look.

> MARGOT. I think that box jelly toxin's gone straight to your head, Sandy.

SANDY opens his eyes, looks around. The women shake out towels to dry off.

> PAULA. You okay, Sandy ?

> SANDY. Oh, yeah, just feeling a bit peckish. (explaining) All the excitement...

> DIANE. Great idea, you can make lunch.

> MARGOT. We always get newcomers to do the first lunch.

> PAULA. It's the tradition.

> SANDY. Oh right. Six lunches coming up.

He smiles at PAULA, turns, trips over BRUCE's esky and heads back to the camp.

> DIANE. Sandy seems like a nice bloke.

> PAULA. Yeah. Bit clumsy.

DIANE (straight to the point) What's he like, you know, in the sack?

MARGOT. Pretty soft I imagine.

PAULA. He's a very sensitive man.

MARGOT. Sounds boring Paula.

PAULA. No- he is. It's unusual to find a man who's in touch with his feminine side.

MARGOT. Yes, but you don't want to get too bound up with him financially. You're not married. . . yet. . . so in the meantime, get everything in writing, darling, that's my advice.

DIANE. Margot, they're in love.

MARGOT. Love doesn't pay the rent.

PAULA. Margot, I'm not after his money, I can look after myself.

MARGOT. Oh, yes, but this band thing. . .

PAULA. It's something I need to do, Margot. We may not succeed, but I just want to be able to say- at least I've tried, you know. With singing I get a real satisfaction.

MARGOT. Yeah, but what about the audience?

FLASH CUT TO: Back at the campsite.

16. MEN ON WOMEN   CAMPSITE
BRUCE, SANDY, RAOUL

SANDY wears an apron as he makes lunch. BRUCE and RAOUL lounge around sucking stubbies. BRUCE has set up a kind of throne for himself made out of cartons of XXXX beer

SANDY. What would be your ideal woman be- if you could create her ? Bruce ?

BRUCE thinks. An interesting question. After a moment:

BRUCE. She'd be like me.

RAOUL. What, fat, greedy, and full of prejudice?

BRUCE. Why do you have to be like that ?

RAOUL. (laughing) No- going bald is sexy, man. (patting him on his pate) Means you've got excess testosterone. chicks love that. You could shave some more off (indicating where on BRUCE's head) Show it off more...

BRUCE backs off pushing RAOUL's hand away.

BRUCE. My excess testosterone? You're just jealous.

SANDY decides to head off this A-type behaviour.

SANDY. I think women have a head start in the growth process. It just seems to me, in terms of their approach to life, they *are* stronger than men- and more sensitive.

RAOUL digs the theme. Gives up on BRUCE.

RAOUL. The whole fact that they can have kids. Can you imagine what it would be like to have a kid ?

SANDY. Growing inside you.

RAOUL. Feeding off your body.

SANDY. Making you sick every morning...

RAOUL. But you'd feel so connected to things.

BRUCE is quietly GROANING. Rolling his eyes at this nonsense.

SANDY. I think that's why women are so strong.

RAOUL. (still on the child thing) The pain must be unreal.

SANDY. There'd have to be a new opening. I'm not quite sure- maybe the belly button? (considering his torso)

BRUCE. Oh can we get off this please!

SANDY. Why Bruce, are you afraid of talking about your own sexuality?

BRUCE. Do you mind, I'm having a drink.

RAOUL. Does it still work, Brucie? The old equipment? Eh? It's not rusting up is it ?

SANDY and RAOUL LAUGH.

BRUCE. How would you like a XXXX shower.

SANDY. Do you masturbate, BRUCE?

BRUCE. Oh fergodsake!

SANDY. It's a natural thing.

BRUCE. So's going to the dunny, but do we have to talk about it?

SANDY. Did you know cancer can be caused by lying to your girlfriend.

BRUCE. What!

RAOUL. What!

Real instant alarm.

SANDY. It's true, they've done a study. And it's logical when you think about it. I mean, cause sex has always been bound up with death, right?

BRUCE. Right, yeah. Sex and Death. Right. Good one.

SANDY. I reckon that's why we reproduce- to have this kind of vicarious hold on immortality.

BRUCE. (gives up) Gees-suzz!

CUT TO:

Back on the beach...

17. MR. PERFECT   THE BEACH
MARGOT, DIANE, PAULA

MARGOT. Bruce? Unfaithful? No!

DIANE. (dubious) Never?

PAULA. (too quickly) No. Not BRUCE.

DIANE. Oh yes, didn't you know. I haven't told you this yet Margot but Bruce came up to Toowoomba last Friday.

MARGOT. (genuine surprise) He did ?

DIANE. Yes, I'd just finished teaching, the Grade 8s had gone, and as I opened the classroom door to go home he was standing there waiting, holding a bunch of roses. Without a pause or uttering a word he threw the flowers aside came in, pushed me down on the desk and we had wild passionate sex on a pile of history assignments and I tell you
what- (deep and throaty) it was fabulous.

They LAUGH.

MARGOT. Well, you can have him. I just want a financial settlement.

PAULA. (turning to DIANE) When's Craig coming over?

A slightly uncomfortable moment.

DIANE. Craig and I are... no longer seeing each other.

PAULA. What? finito la musica?! You're joking!

DIANE. (it still hurts) I thought he was playing a lot of night tennis. I should've twigged it was all mixed doubles.

PAULA. Oh Di…

MARGOT. Di pulled her usual trick.

DIANE. Look, it was fine, it's no big deal.

MARGOT. They're never good enough for you Di. Mr. Perfect, that's what your looking for. And let me tell you, sweetheart, there's no such thing.

PAULA. Margot. (ease off)

DIANE. It wasn't like that Margot. I'm not a perfectionist.

MARGOT. She lied.

DIANE. (insisting) I'm not.

MARGOT. You always set your sights too high.

DIANE. Craig and I just... grew apart, that's all. He liked kayaking, I was into abseiling. It was never going to work.

MARGOT. I think you're a bit frightened. You've been on your own too long.

PAULA. No.

DIANE. I don't want a relationship that's going to be a continual battle.

MARGOT. I bet he asked you to marry him and you backed off.

DIANE. He didn't share my concerns, Margot.

MARGOT. He took you to Port Douglas.

DIANE. We just weren't compatible.

MARGOT. I thought you had triathlons in common?

DIANE. For one he has absolutely zero concept of what it's like to live on a planet that's slowly breaking down.

MARGOT. (giving up on her) Ow !

DIANE. Well, Margot, it's my life too you know.

MARGOT. You'll end up an old maid.

PAULA. Keep trying Di. You'll find someone.

MARGOT. No- great mind, body, money, career, all in the one package, let me tell you, they don't exist.

PAULA. Yes, they do- they're called Sandy!

He appears as if on cue. They turn as one.

SANDY. Lunch is ready.

PAULA. (proudly to the others)
See.

CUT TO

18. BOOKS AND THINGS CAMPSITE XMAS EVE
DIANE, PAULA, SANDY

Later that night…a brilliant moonrise and a starry sky…

DIANE is reading under the light from a gas lamp set up in the dining area.

SANDY drifts in with toilet paper and a shovel. He sticks the paper roll on a narrow branch poking out from a nearby tree and rests the shovel against it.

>DIANE. Not a good idea Sandy… someone's sure to trip over it there and hurt themselves.

So he finds a better spot.

>SANDY. What are you reading?

>DIANE. "Friday"

>SANDY. Michele Tournier ?

>DIANE. (impressed) Yes.

>SANDY. That's amazing, I read that only last week. In fact I finished it in the Kombi on the way up.

>DIANE. No !

SANDY. That's fascinating that you're reading that. I know it so well.

DIANE. I just love the whole idea of being lost on an island, and having to hold onto what you thought was human.

SANDY. Yeah, and it doesn't have that narrative structure that you always get. It's nebulous- more spiritual in some way.

DIANE. Oh yes.

SANDY. Cause you keep going into his mind.

DIANE. I know.

SANDY. It's incredible that you've got that. What else have you been reading ?

DIANE. Oh god- I'm reading school books all the time but I'm continually looking.

SANDY. Have you seen the Virago series ? You know- the green covers.

DIANE. Fantastic, oh yes, I've read all of them.

SANDY. (blown away) You've read all of them ! You're the first woman I've met who's read the entire collection!! Did you know there's a new one just come out?

DIANE. (thrilled) No, really ?

SANDY. (getting up) I've got it in my tent, I'll lend it to you.

DIANE. That'd be fantastic.

SANDY passes PAULA as she comes back to the campsite, drying her hair from the nearby bush shower. Wrapping it up in a towel.

PAULA. What's this?

DIANE. You know the virago series?

PAULA. No.

DIANE. They ahm- oh well, never mind. Sandy's read them. I mean I was just so excited when I discovered there was a whole series and really its so rare to meet a man who knows so much about feminist literature.

SANDY comes back in with the book.

SANDY. (modestly) It's my job really.

He hands it to her.

DIANE. Oh wow, thank you. That's fantastic. I'll make sure I read it before we leave.

SANDY. No- keep it, it's yours. Please. My pleasure. Christmas present.

DIANE. I couldn't.

PAULA. (slightly peeved) I wouldn't mind a look, Sandy.

SANDY. There's plenty more in the bookshop, Paula.

PAULA. ...On the way home. It's a long drive.

SANDY. (slight recurring annoyance) We'll probably have to fly.

PAULA feels wounded by that. Her fault. Again. DIANE now feels slightly uncomfortable

DIANE. Look...er...I really have plenty to finish *"Friday"*...

Handing the latest Virago book back, but he resists. Pushing it back to her, definite.

SANDY. (warming to Diane) Have you caught up with the Shirley Robinson one. . . set on a farm, yet not on a farm.

DIANE. Wonderful. It's that juxtapostion of the nebulous and the concrete.

SANDY. Absolutely. I thought it was ingenious.

DIANE. And unique.

SANDY. Poignant.

DIANE. Profound almost.

PAULA. You didn't tell me about this Virago series, Sandy, I'd like to read one.

SANDY. Well, they're just a bit... nebulous, Paula, you probably wouldn't … (like them...)

PAULA. How do you know?

SANDY. It just seems to me the stories you're attracted to are just a bit more, well … I dunno- straight forward.

PAULA. (not hiding the hurt very well) You mean lightweight.

SANDY. No.

PAULA. I read De Bono, I read Marcuse, they're not straight forward.

SANDY. Yes, but at the moment you're reading Tolkein.

He shakes his head looking to Diane. She is also amused. He rests his case. PAULA is sort of stunned. DIANE picks up her vibe and tries to be supportive.

DIANE. I adore books I find them so inspiring. Whereas you Paula, you've got your music, you don't need words.

PAULA. But I do, I've borrowed lots of books from Sandy's bookshop.

DIANE. Oh I envy you.

PAULA. And...I'm a singer, words is what I perform...

She suddenly bursts into another SONG. The B side of the *Twisted Sisters'* first single. At the end of which the others burst into a rousing APPLAUSE.

19. MOSQUITO ISLAND   CAMPSITE   XMAS EVE
BRUCE, MARGOT, DIANE, PAULA, SANDY

BRUCE comes over to join them with a stubbie in hand, APPLAUDING vigorously- one hand slapping the tinnie.

BRUCE. Go Paula. The new Joni Mitchell...

MARGOT. That was beautiful Paula, thank you.

DIANE. Definitely going to be a hit.

PAULA blushes a little under all the praise.

MARGOT brings over a Scrabble Board and starts setting it up on the folding table.

MARGOT. Alright everybody, get your mental sandshoes on. Capricorns versus the rest.

LOW THUNDER OFF.

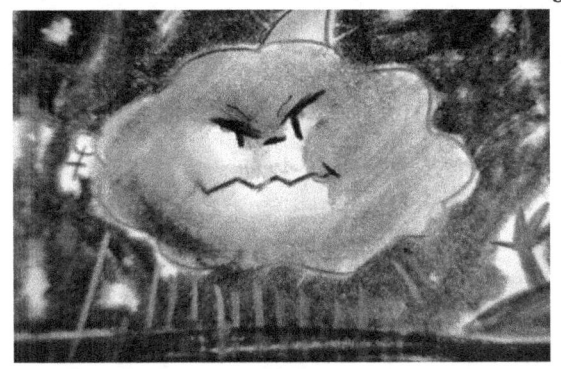

MARGOT. Oh, a bit of lightning about- that'll clear the air.

BLACKOUT.
20. NIGHT GAMES   CAMPSITE   XMAS EVE (NIGHT)
BRUCE, MARGOT, DIANE, PAULA, SANDY, RAOUL

An hour later it's pouring.

They're all huddled under a hastily rigged up tarp in the dining area, seated around the scrabble board.

MARGOT, BRUCE and DIANE have sensible raincoats, RAOUL still has only his t-shirt made from Chux material and pair of tatted shorts.

PAULA and SANDY, with most of their gear lost in the accident, are wearing garbage bags with three holes cut out: two for the arms and one to stick their head through.

Despite the rain, the mood remains jolly. They're singing Xmas carols accompanied by Raoul on Ukulele- while he contemplates his next scrabble
move.

As the chorus of *"Deck the Halls with Boughs of Holly"* comes to an end:

>PAULA. It's absurd isn't it? Singing all those European Christmas carols with holly and snow in them.

>SANDY. What about a punk Xmas carol, Paula ?

>PAULA. Don't know any.

>SANDY. Come on- what would the Sex Pistols have done with "*Holy Night*"

SANDY starts singing *"Holy Night"* à la Syd Vicious. The others laugh.

>RAOUL. (checking his letters) Can you have "biro"

>BRUCE. Don't be a dickhead, Raoul.

>RAOUL. Why not ?

>DIANE. It's a *brand* name.

>RAOUL. No it isn't. It's a writing instrument.

>MARGOT. Raoul, in seven years of playing scrabble together we've never allowed "biro."

>BRUCE. Pass us the rollies, will you Raoul.

RAOUL throws over a packet of Drum.

DIANE reaches into her school bag and produces a blackened lung suspended in formalin in a glass jar.

>PAULA. Good god, what's that !?

>DIANE. A smokers lung.

>BRUCE . Do we have to ?

>DIANE. I use it for my Grade eights. Just a little reminder.

>BRUCE. I'm surrounded by wowsers.

>PAULA. (starting an egg timer) Come on Raoul, three minutes, mate

DIANE has been flicking through a photo album.

>DIANE. Ah- here we all are.

They crowd around for a look.

>MARGOT. That's Xmas Eve isn't it, last year ?

>PAULA. New Years I think, there's a bottle of that dreadful pink champagne Raoul bought.

>DIANE. That's right, we bought a dozen because Raoul wanted the free
>umbrella.

>MARGOT. I had a headache for weeks.

>BRUCE. (spotting him in the group shot) Hah George ! What a show pony.

RAOUL feels immediately uncomfortable. Refuses to look. BRUCE starts teasing.

BRUCE. Looks like he stuck a choko down his y-fronts.

MARGOT. I never liked the way George took his clothes off all the time. There were children over that year.

BRUCE. Look at George, Raoul.

RAOUL. (glumly studying the scrabble board) I've seen it. (beat) Can you have "slut" ?

MARGOT. Certainly not.

DIANE. It's slang, Raoul.

RAOUL. I'm sure I've seen "slut" in the dictionary.

PAULA. Well look it up then.

RAOUL. Well stop the clock.

BRUCE. We can't stop the clock- it's an hour glass.

SANDY. You can turn it on it's side.

RAOUL. I wish we could play Trivial Pursuit.

BRUCE. We can't play Trivial Pursuit.

PAULA. Why not?

BRUCE. Because Margot's read all the questions.

MARGOT. I have not !

BRUCE. Margot, I've seen you systematically going through the cards.

RAOUL. How trivial.

MARGOT. That doesn't mean to say I remember them all.

BRUCE. (under his breath) True. (sadly)

SANDY. Look, do we have to play games at all!?

21. THE ART OF CONVERSATION   XMAS EVE (NIGHT)
BRUCE, MARGOT, DIANE, PAULA, SANDY, RAOUL

They turn as one and regard SANDY with blank incomprehension.

SANDY. Ever since I arrived here it's been one goddamn competitive struggle after another! I mean, you're obsessed! Obsesssed with games!

DIANE. There's no need to swear, Sandy.

MARGOT. But games are fun. That's what we come here for- to have fun.

SANDY. Yes, but it's like the only way you can relate to each other is through some kind of ...competition.

MARGOT. So- what, Sandy, what are you suggesting we do? There's no television, no radio.

SANDY. They're just as bad.

PAULA. Sandy likes talking. Exchanging ideas.

They collectively regard him as some kind of alien.

SANDY. Well, yes, why not? We... we could try talking for a change.

BRUCE. You're out of your mind.

MARGOT. But we are talking to each other, aren't we? Now. We're talking.

SANDY. NO! Now we're just arguing. That's not talking. That's just...another form of competition.

As a teacher and therefore the only other intellectual present DIANE does have some sympathy.

DIANE. What would you like to talk about, Sandy?

PAULA. (sending him up) Perhaps he'd like to discourse on the use of the non-personal pronoun in the works of Simone De Bouvoir

SANDY. (appealing) Paula I ...

MARGOT. I'm afraid you've lost me.

DIANE. I think she's joking, Margot.

MARGOT. Oh...

SANDY. Look. There's this thing called "conversation" right? I know it's kind of a dying artform, but it's how knowledge, real knowledge gets passed on...I mean, god, there's got to be something wider, bigger. can't we just ... share our thoughts?

MARGOT. For how long ?

SANDY. As long as the mood takes us. You see Margot, that's the beauty of it. It's unstructured, it's the antithesis of games. God, Australians, we're just so ... Australian.

PAULA. What do you want us to talk about, Sandy ?

BRUCE. Kombis ?

SANDY. Anything, anything but games.

DIANE. Yeah, Ok, I'm interested. (encouraging the others) Let's give it a try

SANDY. Great, thank you, Diane.

SILENCE.

PAULA. When would you like us to start, Sandy.

SANDY. (slight impatience) Now, we start now!

MORE SILENCE.

BRUCE. I wonder what George is doing tonight?

RAOUL. (exploding) Shit, Bruce, you're just a bloody piss taker aren't you?

MARGOT. (rounding on Bruce also) You can't keep your mouth shut!?

BRUCE. You should talk! God, being married to Margot's like living with the town crier. (to the others) She talked to a store dummy once for twenty minutes before realising it. I know for a fact that she can talk underwater because she nearly drowned one day trying to explain to a friend that she'd dropped the phone in the pool.

PAULA. You're making that up.

SANDY. No No No, that's just vituperation and pointless bickering. I'm talking about meaningful discourse.

RAOUL. Ok you want meaningful, huh? Let's try truth or dare.

BRUCE. Don't get personal, Raoul. You know it always ends in tears. Mostly yours.

RAOUL jumps up and sends the scrabble board flying, before storming off into the night...

LOW THUNDER is heard off, it starts to rain again.

DIANE. Good-one, Raoul, who's going to clean up my scrabble pieces out of the mud?

But RAOUL is gone.

BRUCE. Well, that gives us something to talk about.

MARGOT. Don't push it Bruce, he's close to a nervous breakdown over this George business.

BRUCE. Dumbells ! And wild rice ! A bicycle and a ukelele. I couldn't believe it ! That's all he brought. What use is he to anyone!?

SANDY. (stands to go) On that note I think I might call it a day.

BRUCE. You're not piking out are you?

SANDY. Bruce, I've lost a Kombi, bogged another car which I don't own and am uncertain about the insurance on, I've been attacked by venomous sea creatures, got second degree sunburn, I'm wet and I'm tired... (almost cracking) and I'd like to spend a little time with Paula. Alone.

BRUCE. Ah, come on, it's Xmas Eve fercrissake. We might've eaten all the chops but there's plenty of grog left, the toilet's still working, let's party

SANDY. Paula, are you coming?

PAULA. (still a bit pissed off with him) Is there any reason I should?

SANDY. (reciting)
"While the summer still doth tend upon my state.
And I do love thee;
Therefore, go with me.
I'll give thee fairies to attend on thee.

> And they shall fetch jewels from the deep and sing.
> While thou on pressed flowers dost sleep;
> And I will purge thy mortal grossness so
> That thou like an airy spirit go…

PAULA smiles and melts a little. Aah. He can be so nice.

So Sandy takes her gently by the hand and leads her towards their tiny tent.

> MARGOT. (turning to BRUCE) Why don't you say things like that to me ?
>
> BRUCE. (quoting) "Oh what fools these mortals be." How's that?

He raises his tinnie of XXXX and takes a long swig.

> DIANE. (neutral) Good-night Bruce…

DIANE heads towards her tent.

> MARGOT. Yes, goodnight Di. (also leaving BRUCE and heading for their palatial tent)

As lights come on and off in the three tents.

> DIANE. (off) Night, Paula, Sandy.
>
> PAULA. (off) Night, Di.
>
> SANDY. (off) Night, Di.
>
> DIANE. (off) Night, Margot.
>
> MARGOT. (off) Night, Di, Night, Paula, Sandy…
>
> PAULA & SANDY. (off) Ni-ight !
>
> BRUCE. Happy wet dreams, Sandy.

MARGOT. (off, stern) Bruce! Come to bed !

BRUCE is left alone under the fly. He drains the last of his tinnie, crushes it up and throws the empty towards a growing pile.

MARGOT. (off) Night Raoul.

No answer. BRUCE BURPS. FARTS.

BRUCE. (to himself) Better out than in.

BLACKOUT.

BRUCE. Sandy, Paula, stop that ! (laughs)

MARGOT. Bruce, go to sleep.

22. XMAS MORNING   CAMPSITE
BRUCE, MARGOT, PAULA, SANDY

FADE UP brilliant summer's sunrise.

The rain has stopped but PAULA and SANDY'S tent has collapsed around them.

MARGOT emerges from her tent in a sort of Santa Claus ensemble carrying a small plastic Xmas tree, she RINGS A BELL

>MARGOT. (singing) Jingle Bells, Jingle Bells, Jingle all the way.

>MARGOT. Sandy, Paula, Merry Xmas !

They GROAN and stir awake..

>PAULA. (reacting to the tent)) What ? Oh no! Sandy! Wake up!

>MARGOT. Just a little something from BRUCE and I.

>PAULA. Margot! You shouldn't have.

>MARGOT. Merry Xmas, Sandy.

MARGOT hands them a Xmas present each.

>PAULA. (opening hers) But Margot, I thought we'd agreed we weren't going to exchange Xmas presents anymore.

>MARGOT. I don't remember that.

>PAULA. Last year! When I gave Bruce this... (holding it) corkscrew and you ... (noticing Sandy's gift as he opens it) those tennis balls.

MARGOT slumps. Sprung.

>PAULA. Honestly Margot, this whole Xmas thing has become so commercialized. What does it mean that you give me a corkscrew? What does that say about our relationship ?

>SANDY. (trying to be helpful) It's screwed ?

>MARGOT. Now I feel terrible. God I'm a dingbat sometimes. Talk about a blond moment. If only I wasn't a Brunette.

PAULA. (trying to be positive) It's the thought that counts.

SANDY. Not from what you've just been saying.

MARGOT. No- I'll go and find something else.

PAULA. Margot, please. (stop!)

MARGOT. Come to the salon then before you go back. I'll throw in a facial. You too Sandy, the shave and haircut's on me.

SANDY I rather like ... (my beard, thanks)

He strokes the small goatee he's been trying to grow for years.

23. XMAS MORNING　　　DAY　　　　CAMPSITE
BRUCE MARGOT

BRUCE emerges from their tent. Bleary eyed but frisky. As always. He grabs MARGOT from behind in a mock passionate and embrace.

BRUCE. Margot-

She jumps forward in fright.

BRUCE. Merry Xmas, sweetheart.

Hands her a long thin package wrapped in Xmas paper.

MARGOT. (thrilled) Oh Bruce ! It's lovely. (uncertain) What is it?

BRUCE. Could it be that pearl necklace you're thinking? The string of mikimotos we saw in Kyoto last year?

Fascinated MARGOT feels the length and weight of the present:

MARGOT. (excited) It's certainly long enough, and heavy. (delicious alter thought) Might be gold...

BRUCE, (chuckling in anticipation of the big reveal) It's a *golden* colour.

BRUCE holds a branch of gum leaves over his head. Coy

BRUCE. Don't I get the ritual … (kiss).

MARGOT pecks him on the cheek before eagerly tearing the Xmas wrapping open. It's not easy, BRUCE has overdone the sticky tape.

While MARGOT is thus occupied, BRUCE invites PAULA under his branch.

BRUCE. Merry Xmas, Paula.

PAULA and BRUCE kiss, tentative, loaded. He goes for the lips, she diverts to a cheek- he lingers just a fraction too long...

MARGOT's finally torn all BRUCE's wrapping paper off to reveal a… cricket bat!

MARGOT. Oh Bruce, very funny. Where's my real present?

BRUCE. Look, this is a Gunn and Moore Imperial Willow. This is the best bat money can buy. Even the English team use it.

MARGOT. I know you've got the keys to my new Beemer (BMW) somewhere- is this a game? Where are they ? Am I hot ?

She starts rummaging through BRUCE's knapsack.

MARGOT. (dropping the bag)…are they in the tent ? Am I getting hotter.

BRUCE. You're getting hotter, Margot. I'm getting hotter, we're all hot, let's hit the beach. There are beautiful curling breakers going to waste.

He heads for the beach she follows, refusing to give up.

MARGOT. Bruce, stop it. Tell me where my present is. This isn't funny anymore.

For a moment this leaves SANDY and PAULA alone. A touch awkwardly.

24. XMAS MORNING   CAMPSITE
PAULA, SANDY

SANDY. Darling, I got you an antique tea pot for Xmas. English porcelain.

PAULA. Oh Sandy ! No.

Despite her earlier plea to MARGOT about no presents, PAULA is quietly chuffed that Sandy has thought of her.

SANDY. Trouble is- it was on the roof rack.

PAULA. Oh.

SANDY. Yeah, I checked the trunk before we left the wreckers. It was...you can imagine...the impact when we rolled would have been tremendous. It was just a pile of white chips.

Another uncomfortable reminder of the crash for PAULA. Her fault.

SANDY. So I got you this.

Hands her a medium sized shell, not even wrapped.

PAULA. Oh Sandy, that's lovely. I've never seen one of these on Straddle before.

SANDY. (correcting) Oh no- I pinched it from your Mum's place last night.

PAULA. (appalled) Sandy!

SANDY. She'd hardly notice. There were so many.

PAULA. In Stafford? Our family home...

SANDY. I think it's Polynesian, actually. Or Melanesian. Somewhere up there in the Pacific. Vanuatu maybe.

PAULA doesn't know whether to be annoyed or grateful.

PAULA. The colours are great. And the pattern.

SANDY. Yeah, I thought you'd like them. Reminded me of you.

PAULA. What- a shitty brown, with spots?

SANDY can't help laughing.

SANDY. Of course not. You're luminous. Glowing from the inside. You're ore a pale, greeny blue. With your silken curly hair...

He'd love to run his hands through it right now and she warms to the flattery.

SANDY. And eyes ... that I just (sighs) Get lost in...

But before SANDY can get any worse she fortunately breaks his flow...

PAULA . Well, I knitted you a cardigan.

SANDY. Oh wow !

PAULA. Only- it's in the boot of the Falcon. Sorry. I'll get it later.

SANDY. Are you kidding, you've already given me this holiday. I don't need anything more.

PAULA. Doesn't seem like you're having a very good time.

SANDY. Rubbish, I'm having a brilliant time. Meeting all your old mates from Brisbane. (Rolling his head and hands - indicating a
certain loopiness) Your old gang... (chuckles) Thank god you left this place for real civilisation...

PAULA. You Melbourne boys are so full of yourselves.

SANDY. That's why all we need for Xmas is a damn good pash.

PAULA. That's easily provided.

Their lips hover on the brink, trembling slightly...

PAULA.(certain breathlessness) Merry Xmas, darling.

SANDY. Merry Xmas, Paula.

And they fall the last few centimetres towards each other... until finally: their lips are about to finally collide... just as MARGOT emerges back from the beach, shattering their all too brief romantic moment..

MARGOT. Where's Raoul!? He's holding up the toast.

She reaches into their large esky to extract a bottle of very expensive French champagne.

PAULA. Probably out on a dune somewhere, working the tan.

Just as DIANE jogs in from her early morning sprint along the beach, going into some warm down stretches.

MARGOT. (greeting her) Diane! Merry Xmas !

She goes to get DIANE'S pressie from inside their tent.

>DIANE. (grimly) I don't think so, Margot. The creek's about fifty metres wide.

25. FLOODED IN CAMPSITE   XMAS DAY
MARGOT, BRUCE, DIANE, PAULA, SANDY

>MARGOT. (shocked) You're joking.

>SANDY. After only one night?

>DIANE. It was eight hours of continuous downpour, Sandy. Around here the water table's just below ground level at the best of times. Even our dune is barely a metre above sea level.

>BRUCE. (returning from his swim, drying his hair) Are the cars alright?

DIANE. From what I could see ours are OK but I'm afraid Sandy and Paula's Falcon has been washed about half a mile downstream.

SANDY. Good ! God ! My cardigan !

DIANE. Since it's still close to our side of the creek and since it's upside down, I took the liberty of draining off a bit of petrol. We'll need it to get a fire started.

She puts down the XXXX stubbie that she's carried the petrol back in.

SANDY. Upside down- Geezus ! We've got to do something. Call a tow truck.

BRUCE. No truckie's going to risk going anywhere near that creek 'til the level drops.

PAULA. Well, I guess the car's not going anywhere…

SANDY. It's gone half a mile already.

DIANE. (relax) Then it's still a good mile or so from the ocean.

She starts drawing a mud map- in the sand.

DIANE. In fact we've become virtually surrounded by water. The creek has filled up the swamp behind us and breached the main dune in two places: east of Amity and just here before Adder Rock,

PAULA. So - what you're saying is- we're cut off from the rest of the island ?

DIANE. Both creeks are raging torrents. Even if you tried to swim around their outfalls on the beach, you'd be caught in a rip.

SANDY. Oh god !

PAULA. How romantic. Just like "*Castaway*".

MARGOT. (enjoying the adventure) "*Gilligan's Island*".

SANDY. I think as soon as the water goes down we should get out of here.

DIANE. Don't be a wimp, Sandy, light the fire and we'll have a nice cup of tea.

DIANE gives him the tin of petrol, he starts to pour it on the wood she's gathered under the metal grate they're using for a camp BBQ.

MARGOT. Anyway, it's all connected to the tide isn't it? I'm sure as soon as the tide's out we'll be able to walk out along the beach.

SANDY throws a lighted match at the fire.

DIANE. Careful!

SANDY leaps back but nothing happens.

BRUCE grabs the bastard ball, bouncing it around.

BRUCE. Come on- Optimists versus Pessimists.

Urging them towards the Bastard Ball court.

BRUCE. Look on the bright side, it hasn't rained all day so far. By tomorrow everything will be back to normal. Ah Queensland! Blue skies one day, pretty damn near perfect the next…

Loud CRASH OF THUNDER.

BLACKOUT.

Sound of HEAVY RAIN.

Fade up MUSIC. Fade up HOUSE LIGHTS for

INTERVAL

During which Tim Tams, Xmas Cake (boiled fruit cake) plus tea and coffee are served. The SOUND of RAIN and occasionally, LIGHTNING continues through the entire break…

109

ACT TWO

After about thirty minutes the lights fade on the audience and the sound of RAIN POURING fades up with the lights on stage.

26. STUCK   CAMPSITE XMAS (NIGHT)
MARGOT, BRUCE, DIANE, PAULA, SANDY

It's later on Xmas night and our cheerless group are all huddled back under the fly in their raincoats as a full on tropical downpour THUNDERS down all around them. SANDY and PAULA's improvised garbage bag raincoats looking more inadequate than eve.

Outside the communal tarp SANDY stands in the rain, somewhat zombie-like, repeatedly strikes and throws damp matches at a water logged heap of firewood. As if he's cracked in some way.

For some moments nobody says anything. The only sound is the RAIN and SANDY'S pointless damp match routine.

BRUCE is swotting mosquitos with a ping pong bat.

The SMELL OF MOSQUITO COILS diffuses through the camp. MARGOT has a hat on with it's own built in mosquito net.

BRUCE. Great dinner, I've never had cranberry sauce with just wild rice before. What a hell of a way to end the bicentennial.

SANDY. If I was back in Carlton I'd probably be washing down the roast turkey with a vintage cab sav and a home made cappucino.

PAULA. Well, you're not at home and there's no roast turkey so it's pointless even talking about it.

SANDY. Paula- I'm uncomfortable, I'm being eaten alive by fever carrying mosquitos, every car I seem to touch turns into a wreck... Raoul's disappeared.

PAULA. We're all in the same boat, so stop complaining.

SANDY lifts one side of his garbage bag raincoat to examine the earlier wound.

SANDY. Ahh! Geezus, the blue bottle thing's turned into a tropical sore. Look at that!

PAULA. You're alive! (be grateful)

SANDY. You call this living?

PAULA puts her walkman on. Shutting him out. SANDY is shocked into silence.

MARGOT. Poor Raoul he brought the wild rice and didn't even get to eat any.

Another pause in the conversation. Just the sound of RAIN.

MARGOT. His life's a mess you know, first the restaurant doing badly then George. You shouldn't push him, Bruce.

BRUCE. He's a masochist, he enjoys it.

MARGOT. (flare of anger) Raoul, pain? I don't think so...

BRUCE. (dismissive) Raoul's fine. He's probably swum across the creek, found his way to the Point Lookout Hotel where he's polishing off a couple of ports with Christmas pudding.

DIANE. (ominously) Nobody will be swimming across either creek, Bruce. Not with this rain. We'll be cut off for days.

They defer to her headmistress's authority.

SANDY. Gee-zus!

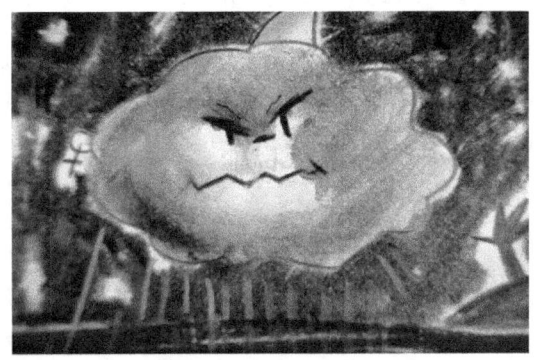

More THUNDER followed by another

BLACKOUT.

27. RAOUL IS DEAD   XMAS NIGHT   CAMPSITE
MARGOT, BRUCE, DIANE, PAULA, SANDY

An hour later….

FADE UP on another glum tableau. Damp and not so happy campers all huddled under a dripping tarp.

Sitting on various boxes and chairs. Rain THUNDERING DOWN all around them. They're finally out of conversation, or any desire to speak.

After a while...

> DIANE. (standing up) Might as well do the dishes and head back to my new book.

She throws a small smile of thanks towards SANDY. But he's too preoccupied with the general predicament.

So DIANE starts picking up various dirty plates, looking around for a dish cloth.

> DIANE. Did I see a chux somewhere- Sandy, is that one near you?

SANDY looks, picks it up and hands it over absently to DIANE.

DIANE shakes it out to flick some mud off

> DIANE. (holding it up) Where did this come from?

> PAULA. Ah (vaguely) I found it on the beach this afternoon.

> DIANE MARGOT (together) On the beach?

DIANE opens it out. The t-shirt shape becomes apparent.

> MARGOT. (aghast) Oh my god, Raoul!

MASSIVE THUNDER, almost directly overhead.

> MARGOT. (stands) I'm going out there. He's in serious trouble, I can feel it .

DIANE. Margot don't be ridiculous.

SANDY. Raoul is dead.

SANDY starts beating the table. Again like he's in some kind of depressed trance. A thumping, dazed rhythm.

SANDY. Dead, dead, dead…

BRUCE. He's not dead, he can't be dead. He's too lazy to die.

DIANE. (agreeing) He is a bit of a wooss. I doubt he'd try anything risky.

SANDY. I can see it now, his head is jammed under a log. His body bloated like a drowned cow.

PAULA. Sandy! Stop it! (trying to snap him out of it)

SANDY. No ! You stop stopping me. I've done everything you've wanted haven't I? 'Came on your stupid camping trip…

BRUCE. Get a grip on yourself, forgodsake.

SANDY. Don't you tell me to get a grip on myself you don't even know me.

BRUCE. If I don't know you then why are you here ruining my camping holiday.

PAULA. Enough! All of you!

SANDY. This is the worst good time I've ever had.

MARGOT. Every other year we've had a beaut time over here.

SANDY. Oh it's all my fault is it ? Is that what you're saying ? I, Sandy Mills, personally brought the bad weather because I'm the nerd from Melbourne.

BRUCE. You got the nerd part right.

MARGOT. I'm going out to look for him. I know he's in trouble We've got a special connection. I can feel these things.

DIANE. Margot, you'll only put yourself in danger. And then one of us will have to risk our lives rescuing you.

BRUCE. I hope you're not looking at me, Di.

DIANE. There's nothing we can do till daylight.

MARGOT. We've got torches, we can search can't we ? This side of the creek at least. We can call out. (calls out vaguely into the night) Cooee ! Raoul, can you hear us ? Cooee ! Raoul....

SANDY. (swaying back and forth) He's dead, dead, dead, dead,...

BRUCE. (fed up with Sandy) Oh forkerrisake !

MARGOT. I'm sorry, I don't care...I just can't sit here and do nothing.

DIANE. Look. As soon as it's light- if the current's not too strong- I'll try and swim across the creek, alright? I reckon the road to Amity should still be open, we can make a call from the public phone box.

MARGOT . I'm coming with you.

BRUCE. Don't be a drop kick. Margot, you can't even swim.

BLACKOUT.

28. SUICIDE?   CAMPSITE   XMAS (NIGHT)
MARGOT, BRUCE, DIANE, PAULA, SANDY

Hours later they're back in their tents. Trying but failing to sleep.

>SANDY. (off) What time is it, actually ?

>PAULA. (off) Three am.

>SANDY. (off) Most people commit suicide at 3am.

>MARGOT (off) He wouldn't commit suicide, Raoul. He's a chef, he loves life. (breaking down)

>BRUCE. (off) I dunno, he's pretty cut up about George.

>SANDY. (off) Actually, Margot a lot of hairdresser's commit suicide, did you know that ? All those women coming in every day, dumping all their problems on you. Complaining about their relationships. It must be very unnerving.

>PAULA. (off) Sandy, go to sleep.

>SANDY. (off) Oh, yes, sleep- as if I'm capable of sleeping in this situation. What if I wake up on the lie-low, floating in a swamp ? What if I bump into Raoul's fermenting, septic body ? I just want to go home, Paula, are you coming with me ?

>BRUCE. (off) No one's going anywhere- we're stranded. Got it? Flooded in. Cut off.

>SANDY. (off) We're all going to die. The kombi was an omen, I should never have driven it north of Bourke Street.

>PAULA. (off) Sandy, if something terrible has happened to Raoul these people are my best friends they need me.

>SANDY (off) (breaking down, sobbing almost) Paula. . .

>PAULA. (off) And I need you… to be strong…

In silhouette inside the tent they move towards each other...while inside her tent DIANE starts singing.

> DIANE. (off/singing) If you're happy and you know it, clap your hands.
> If you're happy know it and you really want to show it
> clap your hands...
> clap your hands...
> clap your hands...

Slowly the others join in....

BLACKOUT.

29. STAYIN' ALIVE   CAMPSITE   BOXING DAY
MARGOT, BRUCE, DIANE, PAULA, SANDY, RAOUL

CROSS FADE TO "*STAYIN' ALIVE*" Mixed with early morning Birdsong...

LIGHTS UP FOR:

SUNRISE...the next day.

The rain has stopped but all that moisture has brought an intense humidity.

"STAYING ALIVE" blares from RAOUL'S ghetto blaster as he pumps his dumbells in the middle of the campsite. Torso bare (having lost his chux t-shirt)

Stirred by the MUSIC, and fairly hungover, BRUCE and MARGOT emerge from their tent, bleary eyed, and agog at the sight of RAOUL working on the body beautiful with his weights.

> BRUCE. (really pissed off) Where the hell have you been !

But MARGOT is delighted, immediately rushes over and throws her arms around him.

> MARGOT. Raoul, thank god, we thought you were dead.
>
> RAOUL. (goes on pumping iron) Careful, Margot, I'm losing count. Two, three…(pumping iron)
>
> PAULA. Raoul, what happened?
>
> RAOUL. Did you miss me ? Eight...nine...

He finishes his set on the tenth pump. And puts the weights down. Puffing lightly, wiping the sweat off his torso with somebody's towel.

> BRUCE. You drongo, you had Margot worried sick.
>
> RAOUL. (at BRUCE) As if you'd give a shit?
>
> MARGOT. (desperate to know) But where were you?

RAOUL helps himself to a glass of left over bubbly and relaxes into MARGOT's banana lounge.

RAOUL. Had to spend all night in the Range Rover. My neck is killing me. (massaging it)

MARGOT. It must've been awfully uncomfortable.

RAOUL. Yeah, I think... I did too many high kicks in that last set. Can you...?

Indicating for MARGOT come and work his neck. She readily does so as he stretches it lightly. Leaning to one shoulder then the other.

SANDY. (anxious) Did you see the Falcon ?

RAOUL. Just the aerial sticking up through the water.

SANDY is poleaxed by the news.

SANDY. Hoh!- geezus.

BRUCE. And the Rover- the Rover's OK obviously?

Since Raoul spent the night in it.

RAOUL. It was only the aircon that made it bearable.

BRUCE. (flabbergasted) You had the airconditioning on ! (disbelief) All night!!!

RAOUL. Well I couldn't open the windows- too many mossies.

BRUCE. What about the battery !?

RAOUL. Huh? (thinks) Oh is that why it stopped ?

BRUCE could strangle him. And moves towards RAOUL with that very intention, but is stopped by MARGOT.

MARGOT. But you're alive, Raoul. That's the main thing.

BRUCE. (gritted teeth) Not for long.

RAOUL. Is there anything to eat, I'm starving.

BRUCE. No Raoul. There's no food left. No chops, no sausages, no bacon and eggs no nothing.

PAULA. There's weetbix and bit of corn relish (left). Plenty of salad…

BRUCE. Like I said, no *food*.

MARGOT. Look, we can go to the butcher's in Amity tomorrow.

DIANE. Margot, I don't think anyone is going anywhere- unless the rain stops and the creek goes down.

BLACKOUT.

30. REAL HUNGER   CAMPSITE   BOXING DAY (NIGHT)
MARGOT BRUCE DIANE PAULA SANDY RAOUL

FADE UP the sound of RENEWED INTENSE TROPICAL DOWNPOUR

Later that night they sit around the dining table under the inadequate fly/tarp in a sort of morose silence.

> PAULA. More corn relish on Wheetbix anyone ?

BRUCE looks interested.

> MARGOT. Don't give him any more he's had his two serves already.

> BRUCE. But I'm still hungry.

> PAULA. Look, it's only 48 hours since we had a proper meal.

GROANS all round. Thanks for the reminder.

> DIANE. Paula's right, a little fasting never hurt anybody.

More GROANS.

> SANDY. (holding it up) Lung stew BRUCE... You're a carnivore.

> BRUCE. Do you mind, I'm just quietly dreaming here of a bridge to Straddle made out of sausages.

PAULA. A big chicken schnitzel topped with a lovely mound of mashed potatoes oozing gravy at *The Danube* in Acland Street.

GROANS

MARGOT. Boeuf Bourgogne and chocolate souffle at *Milanos*.

GROANS

RAOUL. Pan fried baby snapper in a lemon butter sauce. With a crisp rocket and parmesan salad and a drizzle of olive oil.

GROANS

BRUCE. Oh stop it forcrissake !

SANDY. What if we're stuck here for weeks ?

RAOUL. We'd have to eat somebody.

SANDY. Look at that rugby team that crashed in the Andes.

BRUCE. Shocking way to lose your front rowers.

SANDY. It used to happen in Australia all the time... our history's full of Europeans, stranded, eating each other.

RAOUL. I vote for Bruce. He's like a fat pig. We could cut him up into strips, dry him on the tree. Bruce prosciutto.

MARGOT. Oh we can't cook Bruce, I'd be lonely.

DIANE. I don't think whether you've got a partner or not should make any difference.

MARGOT. You're just saying that because you haven't got anyone.

DIANE. (that hurt) What! Well... (bewildered, angry) At least I'm not trapped in a boring marriage with a brain dead buffoon

BRUCE. *Rich* buffoon.

RAOUL. I think we should eat Sandy, he looks nice and soft. Not too much fat.

SANDY. Eat me and you eat my diseases.

The others react, suitably repulsed. BRUCE almost dry wretches.

BRUCE. Don't make me throw up, I can't afford to lose the protein.

SANDY. (pushing him) How'd you like to have chronic thyroiditis for the rest of your unnatural life, Bruce?

DIANE. Muscle meat is the tastiest. I vote we eat Raoul.

BRUCE. Yeah. Roast Raoul. Yum.

MARGOT. Look this is all ridiculous because, I mean, how could we kill anyone anyway? The whole idea is completely absurd.

RAOUL. Oh, you never know. Somebody will probably die soon. Usually it's the weakest goes first.

SANDY COUGHS.

They all look at him.

DIANE breaks the moment with a song.

DIANE. Oh' top of old smokey all covered in cheese I lost my poor meatballs (when somebody sneezed)...

ALL. (except DIANE) Don't sing about food !

So its back to a morose SILENCE. Some night birds are heard TWITTERING off.

>BRUCE. I'm so hungry, I could eat the crutch out of a low flying duck.
>
>MARGOT. Bruce, you're like a broken record.
>
>SANDY. Yeah, one from the *Nazi Beer Hall Collection*...

DIANE perks up into teacher mode. Notices something.

>DIANE. It's stopped.

They all react. My god. It's stopped RAINING.

>DIANE. Come on, everybody- outside.

She leads the way out from under the fly.

>DIANE. (gazing up) Look- there's a fabulous starry sky already. Come on, Bruce, come on Sandy. Clouds are gone!

Mildly curious at this hopeful news, they all move outside the fly to look up at the sky.

31. LOST IN SPACE CAMPSITE (NIGHT) BOXING DAY
MARGOT, BRUCE, DIANE, PAULA, SANDY, RAOUL

>DIANE. Now, how many stars do you think are? (as if in class)...Bruce?
>
>BRUCE. Dunno.
>
>DIANE. Raoul?
>
>RAOUL. (rough guess) A billion...? trillion....?
>
>PAULA. (dreamily) There's a star for every soul that's ever been and ever will be.
>
>DIANE. (still playing teacher) That's a lovely thought Paula. Thank you for your contribution.
>
>SANDY. And a black hole for every rotting corpse.

DIANE sensibly ignores the difficult pupil and moves right along...

>DIANE. Margot?
>
>MARGOT. Hang on, I'm still counting...(under her breath) 47, 48, 9, 50...
>
>DIANE. There's a hundred billion galaxies and a hundred billion stars inside each galaxy.
>
>BRUCE. (impressed) Geeze. That's a lot of undeveloped real estate.
>
>MARGOT. How can you count the number of stars if you can't even see to the edge of the universe.

DIANE. But you can see to the edge of the universe- That's what we're looking at now. Our most powerful telescopes have proved it. That black bit is the edge. Beyond which there's really…just nothing.

SANDY. Funny how life only exists on the edges of things…on the thin surface of the planet, on the edge of this vast dry continent.

DIANE. On the tidal border between the land and the sea.

SANDY. On an insignificant planet, out on the edge of this galaxy we call the milky way...

PAULA. There's probably a group like us having this exact same conversation on a beach right now- on a hundred other planets.

BRUCE GROANS at this palpable nonsense.

PAULA. Of course there is- there has to be. The odds are overwhelming. How conceited to think we're the only intelligent life on the universe.

BRUCE. (up at the stars/proving the point) Hey guys- do think all Collingwood supporters are losers?

RAOUL. She said intelligent life, Bruce. Not Neanderthals like you.

MARGOT. I wonder if they're spunky ?

PAULA. Do you believe in life after death? Do you think we come back as other things?- Creatures....

RAOUL. Yeah, Bruce could come back as a human being.

DIANE. (conclusively) There *is* no life after death, there's only one reality and this is it.

SANDY cracks. Again. For a moment there he was distracted by the speculation. Almost happy. Now it's back to an awful, existential thought.

>SANDY. We're all going to die.

>PAULA. Eventually.

>MARGOT. We can't have been put through all this...this suffering... for nothing. There must be something waiting for me up there.

>BRUCE. Yeah, steak, chops and lots of sausages. With lashings of bacon and hash browns....

GROANS all round.

>BLACKOUT.

32. RAOUL & MARGOT CAMPSITE BOXING DAY (NIGHT)
MARGOT, RAOUL

An hour later the clear sky is holding. The group have broken down into separate couples.

MARGOT and RAOUL have remained behind at main camp site and are playing kamikazee poker.

>RAOUL. You never laugh anymore...

>MARGOT. (laughs) That's not true.

> RAOUL. Jack of spades... (throws it down on top of the pile) That wasn't a laugh that was a cry for help.

She considers RAOUL'S card.

> MARGOT. (raising an eyebrow) Mmm...

Checks through her hand. Throws down her best shot.

> MARGOT. Queen of hearts.

RAOUL is trumped. But plays along.

> RAOUL. You should get a lover, Margot...

> MARGOT. No.

> RAOUL. Have an affair. Go on. There's this new German aerobics instructor at the gym. He's got a torso like a Roman gladiator.

> MARGOT. (insisting) No.

> RAOUL. What?

> MARGOT. I can't move.

She means the cards. He takes the hint.

> RAOUL. Like I said- stuck. In a relationship that's slowly grinding you down.

> MARGOT. I was talking about my cards.

> RAOUL. King of diamonds... (throwing it down) He needs someone to practice his English with.

> MARGOT. Who?

RAOUL. Herman the German.

> MARGOT. Don't be silly Raoul. I can't have an affair, it'd require an entirely new wardrobe.

> RAOUL. Bruce can afford it.

> MARGOT. That's unconscionable.

> RAOUL. You had one… (meaningful pause) once.

It's a painful reminder for MARGOT. For them both.

> MARGOT. I'm sorry darling, but a drunken mistake with you on a night like this four camps ago- does not qualify as an affair

> RAOUL. It might - if Bruce found out about it.

> MARGOT. Don't push it, Raoul, he might look all jolly and 'hail-fellow-well-met' but he's got a weak heart.

> RAOUL. So we wouldn't want to give him any nasty shocks, would we?

> MARGOT. Why on earth would we do that?

RAOUL lowers her cards, stopping the "game" and comes straight to the point:

> RAOUL. Margot, I need twenty thousand to keep La Medditeranné afloat.

> MARGOT. I've already lent you fifteen, and if Bruce found out about that he really would have a heart attack.

> RAOUL. So now I need another 20.

> MARGOT. Well, I haven't got it, darling. I might live in Indooroopilly but I'm not made of money.

RAOUL. You can ask Bruce for it. Make up some excuse.

MARGOT. No. End of discussion. Nyet, Non, Nein Danke.

Again a tense pause.

RAOUL. I don't think so, Margot.

She looks at him in amazement.

MARGOT. You wouldn't dare ! (slight worry) Would you?...

RAOUL trumps her with.

RAOUL. Ace of hearts. You lose Margot...

CUT TO:

33. BRUCE AND PAULA   BEACH   (NIGHT) BOXING DAY
BRUCE, PAULA

On another part of the beach... as the moon starts setting, BRUCE and PAULA are lying on their backs to get a better view of the stars.

Awkward silence.

BRUCE. I'm… sorry I didn't get in touch.

PAULA. I didn't expect you to.

> BRUCE. I got your letter, I ... didn't know what to say- didn't know how to write back.
>
> PAULA. Don't say anything. What's there to say? It was all over in a moment.
>
> BRUCE. (disappointed) A moment?!

Figured himself a better lover than that.

> PAULA. Hardly enough time to think about... what we were doing.
>
> BRUCE. It's just that... Margot is always there, you know.
>
> PAULA. We don't have to talk about it, Bruce. It happened. It's over.

CUT TO:

34. SANDY AND DIANE   (BEACH)   (NIGHT) BOXING DAY
DIANE, SANDY

Elsewhere: some distance away along a beach washed in moonlight ...

SANDY staggers to a halt exhausted, breathing hard, clutching his chest. Then bending over hands resting on his knees.

> SANDY. Oh Di, stop please...
>
> DIANE. Come on Sandy, no pain, no gain.
>
> SANDY. It's the middle of the night and it's like you... you're in some triathlon or something.
>
> DIANE. (come on) Just a few more k's...

SANDY. I think I'm having a cerebral haemmorage. I can feel my head expanding.

DIANE. Are there spots in front of your eyes?

SANDY. (regarding her sharply) Yes!

DIANE. Pain travelling down the right side?

SANDY. (amazed, alarmed) Yes! Yes!!

DIANE. Good, well, the only way to fix that is to keep jogging, come on...

SANDY. Di- please, I wanted to ask you something.

She marks time. Jogging on the spot.

SANDY. What if we *were* trapped here- for months on end ? I mean the whole Robinson Crusoe thing that Michele Trounier talks about. I was trying to image what it would be like.

DIANE. We won't be here for months, Sandy.

SANDY. But say we were... I thought it might be interesting to explore the coupling situations that could arise amongst the group.

DIANE. Coupling situations?

SANDY. A sort of anthropological study.

She regards him strangely.

SANDY. I hope you don't think this is vain- or anything- but I guess I do have a bit of an edge on the rest of them - in the mental stakes- and you're so fit and healthy.

DIANE. Yes ? (get to the point)

SANDY. So- you and me. Survival of the fittest.

DIANE. What are you suggesting ? With my mind and your body we start a master race.

SANDY. No ! Well yes. Actually the other way round...

DIANE is aghast.

CUT TO:

35. MARGOT & RAOUL   CAMPSITE   BOXING DAY (NIGHT)
MARGOT, RAOUL

Back at the camp...

MARGOT and RAOUL have abandoned their game. She's pouring more Bourbon, this is serious.

MARGOT. It wouldn't make the slightest difference to Bruce. You really underestimate him, you know.

RAOUL. How could anyone underestimate Bruce?

MARGOT. Raoul. I'm amazed and appalled...I would never have thought.

RAOUL. I'm desperate, Margot. I can't even pay last month's market bill.

MARGOT. What happened to the rest of the money I gave you?

RAOUL. George took it.

MARGOT. Oh Raoul, you idiot.

RAOUL. I know, I know...shit happens. But... Look, you can afford it.

MARGOT. I thought we were soulmates, Raoul, surely that's more important than any restaurant.

RAOUL. (melodramatic) I'm sorry, friendships mean nothing to me now.

MARGOT. I'm getting a migraine.

RAOUL. Stay there I'll find a painkiller. Mr. Hypochondriac is sure to have something…

RAOUL disappears into PAULA and SANDY'S tent. Where he can be herd rummaging around in their stuff.

MARGOT. (leaning back pinching the bridge of her nose) This always happens when we argue about money.

Suddenly a cry from RAOUL inside the tent.

RAOUL. (off) Hah! (amused/disbelief) What?! (emerging) Hey, look at this. Sandy's got a diary.

MARGOT. Raoul- that's private.

RAOUL. (reading) There's something about you !

MARGOT. I couldn't care less.

RAOUL. (reading) "Christmas morning: Marguerita, the incredibly gauche hair-stylist dressed as Santa Claus and made a complete fool… (of herself)

MARGOT. (snatching it from him) Give me that.

CUT TO:

36. BRUCE & PAULA   BEACH   BOXING DAY (NIGHT)
BRUCE, PAULA

BRUCE and PAULA still lying under the stars. Suddenly PAULA shoots bolt upright. Stung by a sudden, guilty feeling.

>PAULA. I shouldn't even be here.
>
>BRUCE. What on the camp?
>
>PAULA. No- here, with you now. This is…
>
>BRUCE. What?
>
>PAULA. It's not right.
>
>BRUCE. Are you saying- that what happened last year was just…
>
>PAULA. No- I'm attracted to you obviously.
>
>BRUCE. (that's a given) Obviously.
>
>PAULA. But there's friendship you know and...
>
>BRUCE. You're worried about Margot.
>
>PAULA. I don't feel good about it. No.
>
>BRUCE. She knows I have a fling occasionally, it doesn't affect anything. Really.
>
>PAULA. A fling !
>
>BRUCE. (back peddling) Well, no no, not you and I, of course … this is ah… oh - this is different.
>
>PAULA. How is it different?

BRUCE. I want to be your friend.

CUT TO:

37. SANDY AND DIANE (BEACH)   BOXING DAY (NIGHT)
DIANE, SANDY

On another part of the beach lights on SANDY and DIANE.

>SANDY. I was thinking about what you said on the beach before about life being short and we only get it once and it's true, that's so right. We no more know where we came from than we know where we're going.
>
>DIANE. So...
>
>SANDY. So what I'm saying is... I would love to spend some of that time going nowhere with you
>
>DIANE. Sandy, Paula is my best friend..
>
>SANDY. I love you, can't you see that!(damnit!) You're so beautiful and strong, I'm excited by that. Your muscles. Your lean svelt torso... Strength in a woman is so ... so strong.

He reaches out to touch her. She jumps back and delivers a swift kick to the groin.

>SANDY. Aahh! (bending over, in pain)
>
>DIANE. I'm not remotely interested in you and I would never do anything to hurt Paula.

Sandy looks mortified.

>DIANE. Certainly not with a Pisces.

And she jogs off again.

SANDY. (still winded) I'm on the cusp.

CUT TO:

38. BRUCE AND PAULA   BOXING DAY (NIGHT)
BRUCE PAULA

On another part of the beach: lights back up on BRUCE and PAULA.

They lie for a moment in silence, just gazing up at the stars. Suddenly PAULA sounds amused.

>BRUCE. What ?

>PAULA. Nothing.

>BRUCE. No, what ?

>PAULA. I was just thinking...Everyone who's alive today is the result of a...how would you say it- a coupling of two people who once somewhere, somehow, probably loved each other- if only for a moment. That's incredible, don't you think ?

>BRUCE. Well, if it's only for a moment, why think about it ?

They hold a look for a moment gazing fondly into each others eyes before moving slowly in for the big pash...

CUT TO:

39. SANDY'S DIARY   CAMPSITE   BOXING DAY (NIGHT)
MARGOT, RAOUL, PAULA

Back at the campsite MARGOT is now angrily pouring through SANDY'S diary. RAOUL is highly amused.

>MARGOT. (reading) Boxing Day, early. Nose clogged again, couldn't sleep a wink. Felt left nipple, definitely sore, must be

the nylon in the sleeping bag...Afternoon nap: dreamt I went snorkling with Roberto.

    RAOUL. (delighted he's in it) That's me!

    MARGOT. "Patricia"...

    RAOUL. (interpreting/speculating) Paula...

    MARGOT. Rapidly ageing hippie, was pitting all her hopes on one last desperate career gamble. "Stefan..."

    RAOUL. (another easy guess) Sandy...

    MARGOT...Couldn't decide if he was in love with her or just the idea of her.

They break off as PAULA walks in as casually as she can manage. She takes in the strange stares coming from MARGOT and RAOUL. Feeling guilty she reacts:

    PAULA. What? (noticing the diary) What's that?

    MARGOT. (lamely closing it) Nothing.

    PAULA. (mild surprise) You're hiding something.

RAOUL CHUCKLES. Enjoying the whole thing.

    PAULA. Did I miss something?

Raoul LAUGHS outright. MARGOT hits him (with the diary).

    PAULA. What's going on? What's that you're holding?

    MARGOT. Nothing. You haven't seen BRUCE have you?

    PAULA. (too quickly/guilty) Not recently. (diverting with) Have you seen Sandy?

MARGOT. Not recently.

RAOUL. Here he is

PAULA & MARGOT (reacting). Who ?

40. SANDY'S DIARY   CAMPSITE   BOXING DAY(NIGHT)
MARGOT, BRUCE, PAULA, RAOUL

They turn to see BRUCE arriving also as casually as he can manage.

BRUCE. (mock fright) What?

SILENCE. A stand off.

RAOUL prompts MARGOT, nudging her to fess up. She shakes her head. Definitely NO! So RAOUL tries another tack.

RAOUL. You know, Bruce, Margot and I were just reminiscing about that camp four years ago when…

MARGOT. (interjecting, heading him off) Bruce, I'm just writing Raoul out a cheque for 20,000 dollars. Is that OK?

BRUCE. (eyes popping) What!?

MARGOT. He needs it for the restaurant.

BRUCE. What??!!

MARGOT. George has cleaned him out.

BRUCE. What???!!!

MARGOT. Is that all you can say?

BRUCE No! The answer is NO. That's all I need to say.

MARGOT. Don't be so penny pinching, BRUCE

BRUCE. What. No way.

RAOUL. Scumbag.

BRUCE. You expect me to give money to that!

MARGOT. Then I'll draw it on the Curl Up and Dye account. (reaching for another cheque book)

BRUCE. Then it'll probably bounce.

MARGOT. It's *my* money.

BRUCE. No it isn't. None of it is your money. In fact none of it is my money either. (sadly) Not any more.

MARGOT is shocked but recovers.

MARGOT. I'm not sure I follow any of that...

RAOUL cuts across with:

RAOUL. Been having one of your naps, BRUCE?

BRUCE. (immediately guilty) What?

RAOUL. There's sand all down your back.

BRUCE reacts, quickly brushing it off.

BRUCE. Oh- yeah, I lay down to get a better look at the stars. Everyone seems to have their head in the clouds tonight.

BRUCE idly picks up SANDY'S diary from where MARGOT tried to hide it.

BRUCE. (glancing over a couple of pages) What's this?

PAULA. (recognising it immediately) That's Sandy's diary! How did that get out here?

BRUCE. (stopping on a page) Xmas eve, we finally made it to the campsite where we finally encountered Bryce...

MARGOT. That's you, Bruce.

PAULA. Excuse me- I think that might be private...

BRUCE. (barreling on)... the greedy arrogant, sports mad egomaniac lurking like some loathesome carnivore...(breaking off/looking up) Good god this is libelous.

RAOUL. But accurate enough. All the same.

Just as...

SANDY comes in breathless from jogging. Everybody just turns slowly glares at him.

41. SANDY'S DIARY   CAMPSITE   BOXING DAY (NIGHT)
MARGOT, BRUCE, PAULA, SANDY, RAOUL

SANDY. God- I wish there was something to eat. I'm starving.

MARGOT. (flatly) There's no food left.

BRUCE. (disgusted) No food and no trust.

PAULA. (snapping) Where have you been?

SANDY. (innocently) Jogging with Diane.

PAULA. For two hours ! You can barely walk to the coffee shop!

SANDY. Well, no we stopped for a bit and chatted.

PAULA. About what?

SANDY. About her and about … well about you! (flustered) Is there a law against that?

PAULA. What were you telling her?

SANDY. I was telling her how much I loved you

PAULA. (faltering) Oh...

SILENCE all round the others ignore him, SANDY frowns.

SANDY. This holiday has made me realise how much you mean to me.

PAULA melts a little. Her anger and suspicion gone. As they embrace BRUCE reads from the diary.

BRUCE. Daphne...

RAOUL & MARGOT. Diane...

BRUCE. (running on) … has the most voluptuous body I've ever seen. Her breasts protrude like twin peaks of pleasure into the night. She has a pimple inside her gorgeous left thigh. I've been wanting to squeeze it for days.

PAULA reels back.

PAULA. Daphne?

She looks to Sandy for an explanation. He gets it, finally.

SANDY. You've been reading my diary.

MARGOT. You must really hate us, Mr. Mills.

SANDY. Could I have my property back please?

He makes a grab for it, BRUCE tosses it to RAOUL.

SANDY. They're just notes for a novel I've been thinking of writing.

PAULA. What's my name in this novel, Sandy?

MARGOT. "Patricia."

RAOUL. (reading) "Patricia, the neurotic rock tragedy.

SANDY. Give me that. I did not say she was neurotic.

RAOUL throws it back to BRUCE

BRUCE. (reading) Pyschotic. Feeble brained psychotic rock tragedy. Pathetically deluded about her own lack of talent.

SANDY is persists in trying to retrieve it, but it gets passed back and forth before he can reach it.

SANDY. That just goes to show that you haven't read it properly at all. These characters are not real people they're just...just figments of my imagination.

MARGOT. Your imagination's sick. You need help alright.

SANDY. For heavensake! It's just a ... literary exaggeration-dramatic licence. God it's all a joke ! Haven't you people heard of satire?

PAULA. So I'm a joke am I !?

She hits him in the same place as DIANE.

SANDY. Ah!

SANDY YELPS and bends over in pain- just as there's a similar SCREAM OF PAIN off (from DIANE)

DIANE. (off) Ah!

42. ATHLETE'S FOOT   CAMPSITE BOXING DAY (NIGHT)
MARGOT, BRUCE, DIANE, PAULA, SANDY, RAOUL

Everyone looks, DIANE hobbles in with a bleeding foot.

>MARGOT. Oh my god! Your foot !

>DIANE. Ran into the toilet shovel. Stupid, so stupid.

>MARGOT. Bruce, quick get a bandage.

>BRUCE. We haven't got any bandages.

>MARGOT. Well tear something up.

>RAOUL. Lie her down forgodsake...she's losing blood fast.

>PAULA. Get her foot in the air. We need a tournique.

>DIANE. (glaring at Sandy) Some moron didn't put it back where it's supposed to go.

SANDY looks guilty and revolted by the blood. About to throw up. Starts dry wretching...

They all try to lift Diane onto the banana Lounge while holding her wounded leg up in the air, but the banana lounge won't go level, they keep crimping her up inside it to unclick it and lay it flat...

Finally BRUCE grabs one of MARGOT'S expensive dresses, starts to tear it into strips for a bandage.

>MARGOT. Oh no ! Not the Prue Acton.

BLACKOUT.

43. DESPAIR!   CAMPSITE   DECEMBER 29TH
MARGOT, BRUCE, DIANE, PAULA, SANDY, RAOUL

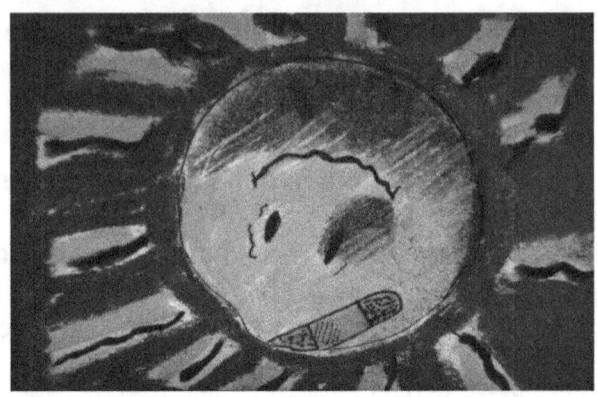

The SUN RISES on a scene of complete shambles. It's raining again. Heavily

DIANE moans in the banana lounge under her raincoat, her leg already swelling badly to double its normal size.

PAULA tries to make her comfortable, mopping her brow with a wet piece of MARGOT'S Prue Acton.

BRUCE looks hungrily at a bottle of tomato sauce, contemplating the contents, then suddenly drinks the lot. Almost throwing up.

RAOUL sharpens the axe on a stone. Over and over again.

MARGOT finishes off her last bottle of bourbon, draining the contents into a glass.

SANDY sits in his improvised garbage bag/raincoat outside the communal tarp, wet and miserable. The exile.

Nothing is said.

The SUN GOES DOWN

FADE OUT.

44. TAX PROBLEM   CAMPSITE   DECEMBER 29th (NIGHT)
MARGOT, BRUCE, DIANE, PAULA, SANDY, RAOUL

Night.

They're all in their tents. Except for SANDY still outside. Still the outcast.

>MARGOT. (off) Bruce, were you hinting at something with that tasteless joke about the cheque account being empty.
>
>BRUCE. (off) It's no joke, Margot.
>
>MARGOT. (off) Surely there isn't a shortage of cash this time of the year
>
>BRUCE. (off) Margot, don't worry about it, there's just a little tax problem, alright ?
>
>MARGOT. (off) What tax problem?
>
>BRUCE. (off) I've been called up for a desk audit.
>
>MARGOT. (off) But that isn't a problem? (surely?)

BRUCE. (off) It will be when they find out seven of our companies are a tiny bit water logged.

MARGOT. (off) What do you mean waterlogged ? Why are they waterlogged ?

BRUCE. (off) Because they're sitting at the bottom of the harbour.

MARGOT. (off) You mean, you've broken the law?

BRUCE. (off) Not exactly broken, no. Just bent a little. So there's now a problem with the back taxes.

MARGOT. (off) How many back taxes ?

BRUCE. (off) About a hundred and eighty thousand.

MARGOT. (off) Well what's the problem? That's not very much.

BRUCE. (off) The problem is we haven't got 180 grand unless I get back to the office tomorrow to sign the contract and pass on the greasy bag...

MARGOT. (off) Greasy Bag?

BRUCE. (off) The little paper bag that greases the wheels of Queensland bureaucracy.

MARGOT. (off) Oh. You mean "bribe."

BRUCE. That's why they call they "Bribey Island" Margot...

MARGOT. (off) You're telling me in other words… we're broke !

BRUCE. (off) You could possibly save "Curl Up and Die"- if you divorced me.

MARGOT finally emerges from the tent. Unable to sleep..

>MARGOT. Why didn't you tell me any of this?
>
>BRUCE. (off) I didn't want to spoil the holiday.
>
>MARGOT. Spoil the holiday ! Bruce, I'm stranded in the middle of a mosquito infested swamp, every stitch of clothing I possess is in tatters, I'm out of bourbon, Di is slowly getting gangrene and now you tell me that in the unlikely event you get back to Brisbane tomorrow - I'm about to go on the dole.
>
>BRUCE. (off) If we get the pipeline deal we can- just possibly- trade our way out of it
>
>DIANE. (off - suspicious) What pipeline deal?
>
>MARGOT. Bruce is tendering to build the pipeline that will pump fresh water straight out of Blue lake into a number of Brisbane reservoirs.

Big reaction from the group. WHAT!!! They all emerge from their tents. This is a direct threat to their pristine holiday paradise.

>BRUCE. Margot, that's confidential commercial information.
>
>MARGOT. In return for which Bruce and number of other developers get a sizable chunk of Straddie's crown land.
>
>DIANE. You're not serious.
>
>BRUCE. This island needs a bridge. Brisbane needs water. It'll create jobs.
>
>PAULA. All you care about is your hip pocket.

BRUCE. There'll be parks, there'll be fountains, nature strips, a golf course, marina, canals, theme parks... I care about the environment. Trust me.

RAOUL. Admit it Bruce, you couldn't give a *stuff* about the environment.

DIANE. This is the last bit of real wilderness left on the entire Queensland coastline and you're going to turn it into another Gold Coast?

BRUCE. What's wrong with that? Excuse me...Wilderness? We're in a wilderness alright, we're starving in the bloody thing. We'd be home now if there was a bridge.

SANDY. You criticise me for not driving in over the creek while you plot to destroy an entire ecosystem.

BRUCE. At least you know if I own the land I'll be conserving as much of its I can.

DIANE. Nobody owns the land. The land owns *US*! We've understood *NOTHING* ! We've learnt nothing about the land in *200 YEARS* !

BRUCE. Crap. We've learnt how to mine it, dam it, drain it, landscape it, build freeways through it …

The others retreat back to their tents. BRUCE is left with SANDY.

BRUCE. Bloke's gotta make a crust.

The sun sets on another gloomy day…

BLACKOUT.

Sound of MORE RAIN.

45. PACKET OF CHIPS   CAMPSITE   DECEMBER 30th
MARGOT, BRUCE, DIANE, PAULA, SANDY, RAOUL

Dawn breaks on the seventh day. The sun painfully pushing the moon away.

An exhausted PAULA wearily marks it off on the tree. Like a prisoner in her cell.

By now they're hardly moving. They lie about in postures of exhaustion.

SANDY is going through a garbage bin hunting for scraps of food left on dirty serviettes etc.

RAOUL is eyeing off DIANE'S smoker's lung.

>RAOUL. I wonder what lung stew does taste like?

SANDY heaves and almost throws up.

BRUCE slinks in at the rear. His mouth is full of chips, he hides the packet under his shirt. But the chips crackle as he gorges them down.

>MARGOT. Bruce, where have you been What's that in your mouth? Are you eating something ?

BRUCE MUMBLES incoherently. His mouth chock a block with crumbly chips.

They all perk up, converge on him.

>RAOUL. What is it?

>ALL. He's got food. He's eating something...

>BRUCE. Get back, get back or I'll scoff the lot.

He holds what's left of the bag of chips threateningly close to his mouth. The rest slink back

>MARGOT. He's got a packet of chips.

>RAOUL. (hungrily spotting the packet) Salt and Vinegar

>BRUCE. I found them washed up on the beach.. They're mine !

>MARGOT. Don't be silly Bruce, half of them are mine. I'm your wife.

>BRUCE. I thought you wanted a divorce.

MARGOT. I'm still entitled to fair share.

BRUCE. (drawing a line across the sand)) Come over that line anyone of you and I'll eat the lot !

SANDY. Oh this is silly, give us a chip forgodsake (moving forward).

BRUCE starts munching frantically. SANDY stops.

PAULA. Bruce, you have to share them. It's not fair.

DIANE. (delirious) Bruce McKenzie, bring those chips out the front and put them on my desk immediately.

BRUCE is taken by surprise, takes a step forward as if hypnotised by DIANE'S headmistress persona, RAOUL seizes the opportunity and lunges for the chips..

BRUCE. (recovering and again threatening to gorge himself)) Get back, get back..

PAULA. (to Raoul) Get back, you idiot !

She's pulling SANDY back behind the line as well.

MARGOT. He'll eat them for sure...

They all rear back from BRUCE's line.

BRUCE. Right, now get me a chair.

They look at each other incredulous.

BRUCE. (again pressing the chips close to his mouth) Come on, come on...

They snap to. MARGOT brings him a chair. He rewards her with half a chip. Which she hungrily devours and steps back behind the line.

BRUCE sits, makes himself comfortable.

> BRUCE. Now Sandy, a tinnie, if you wouldn't mind...
>
> SANDY. Yes of course, of course....anything.

At least they still have plenty of XXXX.

SANDY gets him a tinnie and gets half a chip in return which he monsters, swallowing hard.

> MARGOT. Bruce, that beer'll just make you hungry.
>
> BRUCE. Shut-up! (relishing his new power) I'll have a ciggie, thanks Paula.

PAULA doesn't move. BRUCE eats another chip. There's shock all round.

> PAULA. Alright, alright.

She gets him a smoke, lights it for him.

> BRUCE. Now, Raoul, wash my feet.

RAOUL moves tentatively forward, removes one of BRUCE's thongs, contemplates the filthy feet confronting him and immediately hurls the thong into the bush.

> RAOUL. You've got to be joking!
>
> BRUCE. You want to see something funny? (eats another chip)
>
> MARGOT. You bastard Bruce.
>
> BRUCE. Yes, that's right, I'm a bastard. And you know what Bastards play?

OUTRAGE all round...

BRUCE grabs the basket ball, grinning malevolently, ball in one hand chips in the other…

46. BASTARD BALL   CAMPSITE   DECEMBER 30th
MARGOT, BRUCE, DIANE, PAULA, SANDY, RAOUL

>BRUCE. OK, OK I'll be fair. Whoever wins... eats the chips, Whoever loses... gets to watch.

More OUTRAGE.

>BRUCE. I'm the captain so… I'll have Paula… and Raoul.

>MARGOT. Oh thank you very much.

>SANDY. Yeah, how are we supposed to play with a cripple in our team?

DIANE struggles to her feet, intending to hop/limp over to take her place on court.

>DIANE. Come on we'll show him. I love thrashing Bruce.

She gets up takes a takes a few awkward steps before collapsing.

>SANDY. (pulling her to her feet/desperate) Get up you wimp, get up...come on. I'm starving.

>MARGOT. She's injured and in pain! Can't you see that!?

>SANDY. (to Diane) Get up! (back to BRUCE) You animal Bruce,
>(to Diane/urging her forward) Up up !

MARGOT helps DIANE up. Who is immediately wobbly on her feet. But determined to play.

>DIANE. (to BRUCE, defiant) Come on you bastard, hit the ball ! Rally for serve.

154
BRUCE. Nunce...

BRUCE goes to hit the ball, but by mistake hits the chips. They scatter everywhere. There's a mad ravenous scramble for them in which DIANE gets crushed and the chips effectively ground into the dust.

BLACKOUT

47. MUSHIES CAMPSITE   NEW YEARS EVE (NIGHT)
MARGOT, BRUCE, DIANE, PAULA, SANDY

FADE UP another gloomy night as the remains of the rain depression continue to drizzle down.

The not-so-happy campers huddle round the remains of a bowl of wild mushrooms and seaweed.

BRUCE is on the outer.

> BRUCE. (plaintively) Is there anymore seaweed ?

> MARGOT. (disgusted with him) No.

She throws him a mushroom BRUCE devours it.

> PAULA. Those wild mushrooms would've been great cooked.

DIANE. I wish I'd thought of it sooner. There's always plenty of mushies after rain around here.

SANDY. Di, I'd like to thank you very much for... (loses track)

MARGOT. (picking up the empty lung bottle) Where's Raoul?

SANDY. Thank you very much, for the ... (pause/slight puzzle) I can't seem to finish my sentence.

PAULA. Raoul gorged himself on mushies and wandered off towards the creek.

BRUCE picks his bat up and stares at it obsessively

BRUCE. Why do we do this every year. I hate camping.

SANDY. No, what I want to say- Di, is, thank you very much for the…for the…

PAULA. Bush tucker. He wants to say thank you very much for the…

SANDY. No, there's a word, another word. Funny how I can't just... (trailing off again)

PAULA. (looking off) Did someone just walk out the door?

SANDY. Thank you very much for. . .

MARGOT. (prompting) Providing...

SANDY laughs. Rolling about.

SANDY. "Providing" the meal.

PAULA. Hope there's no "proviso" on that.

More LAUGHTER. MARGOT joins in the general amusement.

MARGOT. I think we should make provision for Di dying.

SANDY Die Di die Di die Di Die Di...(pauses) God I'm stuck, stuck on a word. We're all stuck on this island. We're stuck on stuffing bloody Stradbroke bloody island. (sudden panic) Where's my hand?

MARGOT. Under your bottom you're sitting on. (laughs)

PAULA. Well what other bottom would he be sitting on? Margot, you really are stupid sometimes.

BRUCE. Bottom of the harbour. I used to be a moderately wealthy man. People have died from eating toadfish. (to MARGOT) It's my fault, Margot, I'm so sorry.

MARGOT. I'm sorry, too, I should never have let you bring that terrible shirt.

DIANE. There's nothing wrong with his shirt. It's glowing, just like that palm tree. The colours are so wierd and holy. God, what am I saying. I sound like Sandy!

An appalling thought obviously.

MARGOT. There are no palm trees on Straddie. You're thinking of the bible.

DIANE. Why not? There should palm trees. People paid to come here.

SANDY. Yeah, I paid a Kombi and a Falcon.

BRUCE I'm sorry, I so so sorry. (pause, gathers himself) Margot, listen to me, you've got to listen to me.

MARGOT. No Bruce you listen to me.

BRUCE. No. I've got to talk to you.

MARGOT. No. I've got to talk to you.

SANDY. Talk, talk talk that's all we ever do.

BRUCE. (shaking Margot) Listen to me.

PAULA. No, you listen to me.

PAULA gets to her feet and starts singing Leonard Cohen's "Suzanne". The others slowly join in. By the end of which Paula is virtually in tears...

SANDY. God. Doesn't Leonard Cohen bring you down.

48. SHARE THE BEAR   CAMPSITE   NEW YEARS EVE
MARGOT, BRUCE, DIANE, PAULA, SANDY, RAOUL

Suddenly there's a WILD JUNGLE YELL off. And...

RAOUL jumps into the space, zinc cream smeared across his face like warpaint. He's gone completely feral- looking like a deranged Tarzan.

In one hand he holds BLINKY, shafted onto the sharp end of the pole from the beach umbrella.

Horror and pandemonium break out.

PAULA. (still weeping from the song) Blinky, he's killed Blinky!

MARGOT. Raoul, you've gone in sane!!!

She goes over to RAOUL, reaching for the bear. He GROWLS and hits her on the head with it. She SCREAMS.

MARGOT. Bruce, *do* something. Raoul's lost his marbles.

BRUCE. (almost in tears) I'm sorry, I'm so so sorry...

DIANE. Raoul, stop it or this will go on your report. Bring that bear here at once.

RAOUL grabs the axe and steps back, bear in one hand, axe in the other.

RAOUL. My bear I killed it.

DIANE hobbles over to RAOUL.

DIANE. Look at what you've become, I'm ashamed of you. Blinky was our friend, a harmless national symbol.

She slaps RAOUL and easily takes the bear off him.

DIANE. That's it, you're expelled. Never darken my school's door again.

And she limps towards the bushes with the bear, intending a decent burial.

BRUCE. Hang on- you're not going to throw it away are you?

DIANE. Bury it. I intend to give Blinky a decent burial.

PAULA. (to BRUCE) Are you insane?

BRUCE. (hungrily) Koalaburger.

MARGOT. We can't even get a fire going...

RAOUL. You don't need to cook it, you can skin it, strip it, hang it up to dry...

SANDY. Koala biltong.

DIANE. Stop it Stop it all of you ! Blinky is a protected species.

BRUCE. Okay. So now there's only eleven left,

MARGOT. (can't do it) He's an old friend.

SANDY. Well, actually, I didn't know him all that well.

DIANE. I can't believe I'm hearing this.

SANDY. We *are* pretty hungry, Di.

MARGOT. I suppose the aborigines ate them.

DIANE. Actually they didn't eat them. The meat's full of eucalyptus oil, our digestive system simply can't handle it.

SANDY. It does seem a bit of a waste...

BRUCE. Blinky will live through us.

SANDY. His death will not have been in vain.

DIANE. (hugging Blinky's corpse protectively) Anybody touches this bear and I'm going to the police.

BRUCE. Share the bear, Di.

SANDY. (taking up the mantra) Share the bear.

RAOUL. Share the bear.

BRUCE, RAOUL, SANDY Share the bear. Share the bear. Share the bear.

The men keep chanting and advance on DIANE. BRUCE and RAOUL start their familiar haka routine...

DIANE. (stepping back, grossly outnumbered) I'm warning you- I'll scream my head off to the papers.

The menacing half circle falters in its inexorable advance. DIANE senses a chance.

> DIANE. Yes, that's what I'll do I'll go to *Truth*. I'll spill my guts to the *Courier Mail*. I'll tell them how you lost it. All of you. Your reputations will be in tatters.

The CHANTING STOPS.

> DIANE. Raoul, who'd eat in your restaurant? Sandy, no one in Carlton would go near your bookshop. And Bruce, I can see the headlines now: "Property Developer Abandons Humanity for Haunch of Koala". You'll never sell another time share' in your life !

> BRUCE. (low threat) I don't reckon you'll go to the papers, Di.

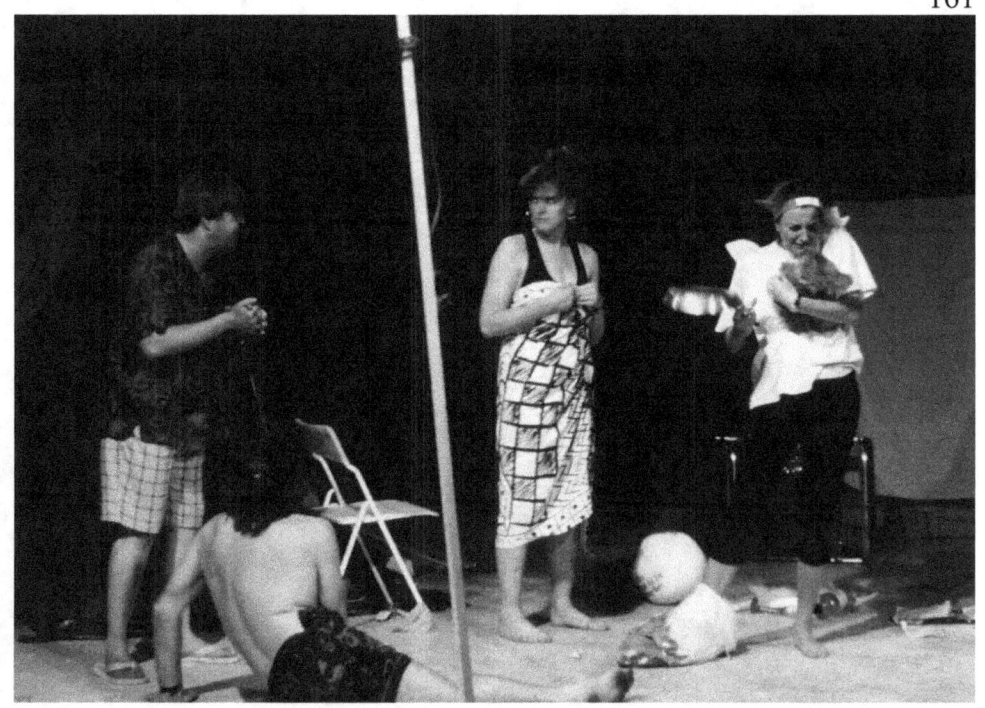

>DIANE. (determined) Oh yes I will....(regarding Blinky protectively)

>BRUCE. Oh no you won't...

BRUCE lunges at her, going for the jugular. SANDY and RAOUL take up the chant again.

>SANDY & RAOUL. Share the bear. Share the bear. Share the bear.

There's a struggle. BRUCE has his hands around Diane's throat, who is still protectively clutching Blinky as she falls backwards into...

>BLACKOUT.

49. AFTERMATH   CAMPSITE   NEW YEAR'S DAY
MARGOT, BRUCE, DIANE, PAULA, SANDY, RAOUL

The next day. Another sweltering sunrise. Intense humidity fuelled by all that rain.

A spot light comes up on a small crucifix sitting in the sand at the end of what looks like a hastily dug grave.

BRUCE MARGOT, RAOUL, SANDY and PAULA stand around it. MARGOT is dressed in black.

>PAULA. Life's so short.

>BRUCE. I don't know what happened, I don't know what came over me...

He breaks down in tears.

MARGOT. We're all guilty.

SANDY. You can't blame the mushrooms. No court would accept that. Mental impairment is no defence for a crime like this.

RAOUL. I just never thought it would end like this.

SANDY. Well, anyway, Di got what she wanted.

BRUCE. We can't let this get out you know, Christ, if the papers *did* hear about it.

Suddenly a HUSKY voice is heard off.

DIANE. Has anyone seen my pegs?

DIANE enters still limping. She carries a sprig of eucalyptus. Her foot bloated out about three times it's previous size from the raging infection.

Her throat is now wrapped in another improvised bandage, hiding the bruises from BRUCE's near strangulation attempt.

> PAULA. Oh, ah- Sandy have you seen the pegs?
>
> SANDY. I think we lost them in that last storm.
>
> PAULA. We'll buy you some new ones Di.

DIANE lays the sprig of eucalyptus leaves on the grave.

> DIANE. (husky) Blinky would've liked these.

A moment of silence.

> MARGOT. So, now, who'll bring what next year? Can I put you down again for the breakie stuff Paula?
>
> PAULA. Oh, ah I think we're going to Sandy's parents' place next year, aren't we Sandy ? (nudging him)
>
> SANDY. What ? Oh yeah … They live in Wonthaggi.

MARGOT. Diane? Do you want to take on the breakfast things?

DIANE. (definitive) I won't be coming back to Straddie, Margot.

BRUCE. (Oh come on!) You're not put off by a drop of rain, and a bit of hardship? Next year I'll bet the weather's perfect.

DIANE. Good-bye, Bruce. I can't say it's been nice knowing you.

That sounds a bit final. BRUCE is genuinely shocked.

BRUCE. Huh...? (flummoxed)

MARGOT. What about you Raoul, will I put you down for the meat again?

RAOUL. Yeah, yeah, any thing you say, Margot. Meat. Fish...flying ducks...

Awkward silence. They look around at the debris of the camp.

SANDY. How long did they say the barge would be ?

DIANE. Can't be soon enough for me.

MARGOT. How long have we been here ?

SANDY. Seems like an eternity.

BRUCE. Eight days I think.

PAULA. I think it was nine.

RAOUL. Yes, yes it was nine.

MARGOT. (thrilled)) Then it's new years day!

BRUCE. God we almost forgot.

Delighted he and MARGOT break out the party hats and whistles that they always bring. People reluctantly put them on.

SANDY resists

>MARGOT. Come on we do this every year, Sandy.
>It's an old Straddie tradition.

They stand around feeling foolish.

>MARGOT. (blowing a whistle) Happy New Year everyone !

>ALL. (half heartedly))
>Happy New Year.

Silence.

>PAULA. (sings) Should old acquaintance...

They all slowly join in SINGING

ALL ...Be forgot For the sake of old angsyne...
Should old acquaintance be forgot
For the sake of old angsyne...
(etc.)...

Which segues into a really up beat number like "Why Do Birds Sing...."
That grows into a joyous celebration of their friendship and shows a
physical (if not completely mental) reconciliation.

                                                FADE TO BLACKOUT

THE ORIGINAL CAMP 1983/84

Caz Howard, Paul Davies
Happy Campers

The communal tent

Bastard Ball

The Flood

More Flood

Wet Camp

Wet Camp

CRITICAL RECEPTION

THE MELBOURNE TIMES

Vol. 23 No. 45 — 237 RATHDOWNE ST., CARLTON 3053. PHONE: 663 6977 — 23 November, 1988

ON SHIFTING SANDSHOES
Theatreworks
14 Acland Street, St Kilda
Review: CHRIS BOYD

PAUL Davies has finally cracked the big one. The man who turned sitcom into sitfarce has crafted a brilliant new play. Prior to this one, Davies relied heavily on over-the-top staging to cover for a basic lack of material.

In *Living Room*, we wandered round a beautiful old mansion. *Storming St Kilda by Tram* was performed on the 69 tram. When Davies risked a straight comedy without gimmicks, *Last Train to St Kilda*, it was a Dud-with-a-capital-D.

On Shifting Sandshoes, however, stands on its own merits; its a fine comic script. The play tells the story of a group of five old friends who holiday together every Christmas on Stradbroke Island.

This year two arrive without partners. Raoul's boyfriend has run off with a frigate load of Norwegian sailors, while Diane hasn't found a man who can keep pace with her liberated athleticism.

Margot, proprietor of a hairdressing salon called "Curl Up and Dye", is married to Bruce, a neanderthal Queensland property developer. The only thing they have in common is a joint cheque account! Margot lives on bourbon and Berocca.

The fifth friend, Paula, a southerner, has brought her new boyfriend with her. Sandy is an archetypal Carlton wimp. He is intelligent, sensitive, and fragile to the point of neuroticism.

The first half of the play is like a burlesque, eighties version of Michael Gow's play *Away*. The games, the intrigue, the bitching and the rituals are all finally drawn. These alone would add up to an entertaining evening.

The play, however, has a twist in its tail. The second half is a Gothic, mushroom-induced nightmare. Heavy rain cuts the group off from the rest of the world. Food is scarce. The holiday becomes a struggle for survival!

On Shifting Sandshoes is tightly acted. Raoul, in particular, is beautifully played by David Swann. Brian Nankervis, better known to the world as Raymond J Bartholomeuz, plays Sandy. Rosie Tonkin's Paula is shyly attractive.

Several of the best jokes are borrowed , but who cares? This is, in my opinion, the comedy of the year.

From left to right and top to bottom, the team from On Shifting Sandshoes – Jean Kittson (Diane), Brian Nankervis (Sandy), Christine Keogh (Margot), David Swann (Raoul), Rosie Tonkin (Paula), Ross Williams (Bruce).

THE AGE

A camping holiday that goes wrong

REVIEW
Theatre
LEONARD RADIC

On Shifting Sandshoes by Paul Davies. (TheatreWorks, Acland Street, St Kilda).

PAUL DAVIES' new play for TheatreWorks — his fifth for the company — is set on Stradbroke Island east of Brisbane. It is, one gathers, a quiet idyllic spot populated by holidaymakers, campers, and 13 blue koalas — the last of their kind.

Well, at the beginning of the play there are 13. But after interval their numbers are reduced to 12. For thanks to a series of misunderstandings and disasters — flash flooding, a car breakdown, confusion about the culinary arrangements, and so on — Davies's six characters find themselves marooned for nine days on the island over Christmas without food or drink. Their choice is either to eat koala and risk prosecution, or to eat each other. They risk prosecution.

From this brief rundown of events it should be obvious that 'On Shifting Sandshoes' is not exactly incisive or innovative theatre. It breaks no new ground; it sets no trends. No one need worry that their concentration will be over-stretched, or that they will be asked to do anything more than sit back and laugh.

Yet as light comedy-farce it works well enough if you don't think too closely about the contrivances of plot, and why and how it is that the six characters spend so long on the island completely out of contact with other humans.

Like Michael Gow's 'Away', which it resembles at a number of points, it is a closely observed play about the the rituals of the Australian Christmas holiday, only stripped of the Shakespearean resonances and overtones which helped to make made 'Away' such a runaway success.

The characters — two couples and two oddball individuals — are familiar and recognisable types. Friends for years, with a background in schoolteaching, hairdressing, property development and running a restaurant, they have come to Stradbroke, as their annual habit, to lie in the sun and give their nerves a rest. Instead they find themselves stressed beyond endurance. The scholarly Sandy sums up the experience for all of them when he says from under his plastic raincoat, while the rain thunders down: "This is the worst good time I've ever had."

If there are any subtleties in the script, neither the director Mark Shir-refs nor the actors locate them. Still, the laughs come freely, thanks in the main to three of the performers: Ross Williams, a gruff and dominating property developer, David Swann, a gay and narcissistic restaurateur, and Jean Kittson, a fitness fanatic who spends most of her time on Stradbroke not being part of the group.

The cast of 'On Shifting Sandshoes', from left: front, Rosie Tonkin, Ross Williams; middle, Christine Keogh, David Swann; top, Jean Kitson Brian Nankervis.

THE AUSTRALIAN FINANCIAL REVIEW

Friday, December 9, 1988

Interesting fare is home-grown

IT'S often said that Australian writers have to live in Sydney to make a living, but Melbourne must surely offer *some* encouragement. For the second time this year virtually every theatre in Melbourne is performing contemporary Australian work.

On Shifting Sandshoes (TheatreWorks St Kilda until December 17) is one in an impressive line of clever, satirical comedies by TW stalwart Paul Davies.

Arguably the funniest show in town at present, it concerns an oddly assorted sextet which takes its Christmas and New Year holidays each year on Stradbroke Island. This year, things go horribly wrong. First, there are newcomers on the scene who can't cope with the group's rituals; then it rains for a week, effectively flooding them out and isolating them from civilisation. Davies extracts some very sharp humour from their ensuing struggles.

It's a shade contrived (this becomes a metaphor for the survival of the species itself, thanks to the presence of a fanatically fit biology teacher) but as pre-Christmas farce goes, it works pretty well.

GEOFFREY MILNE

Eats, Arts and Entertainment

The Emerald Hill, Sandridge and St Kilda Times

From left to right and top to bottom, the team from On Shifting Sandshoes – Jean Kittson (Diane), Brian Nankervis (Sandy), Christine Keogh (Margot), David Swann (Raoul), Rosie Tonkin (Paula), Ross Williams (Bruce).

First class comedy

ON SHIFTING SANDSHOES
Theatreworks
14 Acland Street, St Kilda
Review: CHRIS BOYD

THEATRE

PAUL Davies has finally cracked the big one. The man who turned sitcom into sitfarce has crafted a brilliant new play. Prior to this one, Davies relied heavily on over-the-top staging to cover for a basic lack of material.

In *Living Room*, we wandered round a beautiful old mansion. *Storming St Kilda by Tram* was performed on the 69 tram. When Davies ticked a straight comedy without gimmicks, *Last Train to St Kilda*, it was a Dud-with-a-capital-D.

On Shifting Sandshoes, however, stands on its own merits, its a fine comic script. The play tells the story of a group of five old friends who holiday together every Christmas on Stradbroke Island.

This year two arrive without partners. Raoul's boyfriend has run off with ian sailors, while Diane hasn't found a man who can keep pace with her liberated athleticism.

Margot, proprietor of a hairdressing salon called "Curl Up and Dye", is married to Bruce, a neanderthal Queensland property developer. The only thing they have in common is a joint cheque account! Margot lives on bourbon and Berocca.

The fifth friend, Paula, a southerner, has brought her new boyfriend with her. Sandy is an archetypal Carlton wimp. He is intelligent, sensitive, and fragile to the point of neuroticism.

The first half of the play is like a burlesque, eighties version of Michael Gow's play *Away*. The games, the intrigue, the bitching and the rituals are all finally drawn. These alone would add up to an entertaining evening

The play, however, has a twist in its tail. The second half is a Gothic, mushroom-induced nightmare. Heavy rain cuts the group off from the rest of the world. Food is scarce. The holiday becomes a struggle for survival!

On Shifting Sandshoes is tightly acted. Raoul, in particular, is beautifully played by David Swann. Brian Nankervis, better known to the world as Raymond J Bartholomeuz, plays Sandy. Rosie Tonkin's Paula is shyly attractive.

Several of the best jokes are borrowed...but who cares? This is, in my opinion, the comedy of the year.

No Yuppie Is an Island

It is a joy to walk into a theatre space that has been totally transformed for the purpose of a play.

Theatreworks, for their most recent production of *On Shifting Sandshoes*, have radically converted the Church Hall in which they perform into a complete Queensland holiday beach spot.

The tables and chairs and velvet drapes are gone and in their place are tents, banana lounges, director's chairs, a barbecue, tropical bushes, a camp fire, an impressive oceanic backdrop and a large draped sheet that surrounds the beach spot connecting it to the mainland.

The immediate sensation is one of all encompassing calm that places you right in the middle of the camp site. The lighting and sound also provides the audience with the appropriate aural and visual stimulus necessary for such a complete theatre design. Even the programmes were in the shape of a sun hat.

So the scene is set for the annual gathering of a group of six yuppies at Stradbroke Island over the Christmas-New Year period. They are cut off from civilization (Brisbane, well?) by 30 kilometres of Commonwealth road in a pathetic attempt to be adventurous and to live a little. And they try!

There's Bruce the beer-swilling-chauvinist-land-developer who ritualistically gives meaningless presents like "a fair dinkum willow cricket" bat to Margot, his ocker wife. She romps around the camp site clad in designer raincoats and is not amused.

There's Bruce's old university mate, Roul, a sleazy queen who leaves his epicurean attire at home for a single Balinese batik robe. Roul spends most of his time pumping iron, dreaming of tofu pie, sunbaking and making interminable conversation about his exlover, George, who ran away with a Norwegian bombshell. Roul is as bland as beige carpet and just as twisted.

Then there is Paula. She has a bobbed haircut, large geometric earrings and a wimpy post-modern boyfriend, Sandy. He is a sad reminder of sensitivity gone too far. Sandy is unable to set up a tent, drive a car safely or walk ten yards without contracting some allergy. Watch very closely for his lip. On it is plastered the largest cold sore known to medicine.

Last, but not least, and probably the least interesting, is Diane. She is a frustrated young spinster teacher who devotes her energies to jogging, reading Virago and Pritikin diets. Diane is the type who carries health and nutrition programs with her every where she goes and can produce a smoked lung should anyone pollute the air with nicotined fumes.

This year is just like any other except that some things go tragically wrong. Sandy smashes the car on the way. Roul forgets to bring the meat (surprisingly). Rain pelts down, supplies run out and no-one will play bastard ball with Bruce. Margot and Roul reminisce about their blind grope under the tea tree all those years ago while outside Bruce and Paula discuss the possibility of such a grope. Later on in the holiday, Roul is forced to eat Diane's smoked lung, Bruce bribes the holiday makers with a packet of Samboy chips and Blinky the stuffed koala gets slaughtered in a brutal *Lord of the Flies* style massacre.

What has gone wrong this year? Basically the nostalgic attempts of six people trying to have a good time when sadly all the good times have gone.

In *On Shifting Sandshoes*, six contemporary stereotypes are thrown together in an extremely familiar environment and subjected to a series of unfamiliar happenings that leave them all diving for their car keys.

Take along some lotion and bask in some local beach frolicking.

•Maurice Lawlor

'Paula' and 'Sandy' in On Shifting Sandshoes.

Melbourne Observer Star, Melbourne, Friday 2 December 1988, No 83, FREE

IN BLACK & WHITE
ANNA GRECO

A DIRE case of life imitating art? The cast and crew of the now-showing Theatre-Works production *On Shifting Sandshoes*, which is all about disasters on holiday, are being struck down one by one by freak accidents. First, one actress unexpectedly took off to have surgery. Then, another slipped in the bathroom and suffered concussion. The publicist was next to meet with the same fate, when she gonged her head in the theatre's storage room. The lighting designer fell down a stage ladder and injured his leg. And if that's not enough, the production manager was struck by a police car going the wrong way down a one-way street. But still the show goes on, as it must. Bravo!

The Emerald Hill, Sandridge and St Kilda Times

Circulating throughout the cities of Port Melbourne, South Melbourne and St Kilda
10 November 1988   79 Bay Street, Port Melbourne 3207. Phone (03) 646 5040 or 663 0477   Vol. 11 No 42

A 'castable' actor washes up in St. Kilda

Theatreworks in St. Kilda manages to attract some of Melbourne's most adaptable actors. One of the company's latest "recruits" spoke this week with MALCOLM RIDDLE.

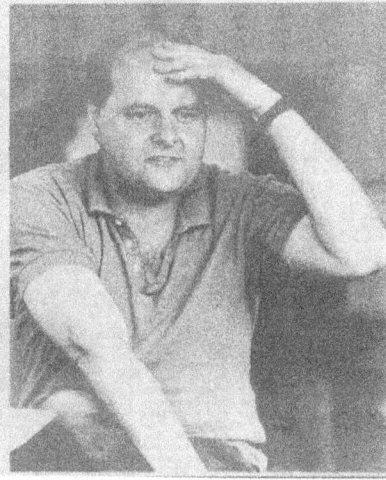

ROSS WILLIAMS pleases people. He pleases directors, playwrights, audiences, the interviewer, and even himself.

Although he'd rather be on stage than suffer an interview, he submits with the utmost goodwill.

"I don't feel I really work for a living," he says. "I consider myself very lucky. That is not to say I don't put a lot of effort into it all. My employers got good value, I want my work to be good, but it's not a case of waking up on Monday morning and saying, 'Christ, off to rehearsal again.' There's nothing else I'd rather be doing, but then I can't really do anything else."

Williams was persuaded to join the Youth Theatre Company in his home town while still a schoolboy, which caused him to turn his back on a possible remunerative career and enrol at The Victorian College of The Arts, where he graduated in 1980. His work since then has included many experiences which have undoubtedly been a benevolent self-education.

He had his pals devised and performed their own shows for such venues as The Collingwood Football Club, and he has ferried up to Comedy Festival and Last Laugh audiences who can dish it out to performers with the best. His skills have frequently taken him interstate, and in true repertory style, he accepts featured roles as well as walk-ons. "If you had blinked, you would have missed me in the last Melbourne Theatre Company Shakespeare season," he quips.

Williams is remembered more recently for roles in And The Big Men Fly at MTC, a part he thoroughly enjoyed, and in Away for Playbox, which was a runaway success for playwright Michael Gow.

He was also one of the team of the ill-fated production of Manning Clark's History of Australia. "There was a germ of a show waiting to get out of that one," Williams says. "But I must say it was something to remember being part of Australia's biggest theatrical flop, mainly because of the spirit of the cast and the dedication of the people involved; a truly memorable experience."

Williams' chameleon-like capacity for varying roles was at work in a sinister Jack The Ripper portrayal five years ago in Gilly Fraser's thriller play I Can Give You a Good Time which toured in two states. One of his greatest assets is his ability to reproduce accents. One director says of Williams: "He also has the sort of face and body which is eternally adaptable. He can be a murderer or a bus driver. He is eminently castable because of this."

Williams' role in On Shifting Sandshoes is that of an insensitive property developer who is a member of a regular gang of holiday makers going on their annual Christmas pilgrimage to Surfers Paradise in Queensland.

He describes the character he assumes as not having one redeeming feature. He is a tatty character who will always try to cheat and bluff his way to the top, even in a softly ball game. "I do like playing nasty people, whether it's comedy or tragedy," says Williams. "This character is my cup of tea; people like him are by far the most fun to play."

Theatreworks are using this piece for the Christmas season, when people need diversion, and they seem to have deemed it the ideal vehicle.

"Terrible things happen to these people, and the audience will have a great time laughing at their misfortunes."

Director Mark Shirrefs has selected as top cast in Caz Howard, Jean Kittson, Brian Nankervis, David Swann, Rosie Tonkin and Ross Williams. Shirrefs has also directed Swanning St Kilda, By Train, Stowaway, Mona Albert By Train and Breaking Up in Reverse for Theatreworks.

● On Shifting Sandshoes opens on November 18, playing Mondays to Saturdays at 8.30 pm, 14 Acland Street, St Kilda. Bookings on 534 8966.

ENTERTAINMENT GUIDE

Notes of an enfant dangereux

THEATRE

BRIAN NANKERVIS

THEATREWORKS' 1988 Christmas show, 'On Shifting Sandshoes, Surviving the Great Australian Holiday', begins at their Acland Street home next Saturday. The saga of an annual Christmas camping expedition gone terribly wrong has captured the imagination of the headstrong and flamboyant Otis Grodner, current "enfant dangereux" of the St Kilda filmmaking push.

Grodner, best known for last year's psycho-generic sci-fi documentary, 'Woman Pregnant for Fifty Years Gives Birth to a Pensioner', has been shooting in and around the cafes of St Kilda for the past 10 days and expects the film to be released on boot-leg video by 1992. The following excerpts from Grodner's production notes give a rare glimpse into the willy-nilly nether world of contemporary film-making.

The premise: That camping on Stradbroke Island, Queensland, is no different from camping in the Middle East, in Brixton, in a Brisbane lock-up, in Belfast, in the Bronx. Volleyball is power, property is theft, tinned food the supreme paradox of starvation. Smash the primus, flood the campsite, hide the blockout and the feral beast in us all will surface and devour basic decencies. That friendship and nostalgia bloom/die/bloom/die in spiralling, heaving cycles. There are those who remember tent pegs, there are those who choose to forget.

Script Notes: No script. No script, no constraints. No gender-repressed roles from infancy. No straitjacket to bludgeon and blunt the creative spirit. No photocopier. No typewriter.

Storyboard: This is proving to be a headache. Archie C. (Catering) and I cannot agree. I say chalk, he says texta. We must make a decision soon — the crew will not eat any more tofu casseroles. How childish to blackmail me this way! Ring Danube re possible schnitzel scam. Where is Archie from anyway? Jupiter? Mars? Stupid hippie.

Character Notes: Zoe: Silent, oppressive. Raised in a cane-field. Married. Craig for a dare. Enid: Speaks only Latin. Dental technician with a heart of gold. Bruces. Willy: Perky, bumptious real estate mogul. Pedantic and balding, with a penchant for bagels. Allergic to nylon. Cho-Cho: The lender. Brutal and uncompromising, he has organised the past six camps. Short term memory is shot. Craig: An enigma. George: An idiot.

Story Line Ideas: George, Zoe, Enid, Craig, Cho-Cho and Willy the Geek arrive on Stradbroke at sunrise, Christmas Eve. Enid and Zoe re-enact the landing of the first fleet and are speared by George. They survive and Craig builds a raft which Cho-Cho burns in a crazed, euphoric stupor. Out of control fire destroys youth club auto tent nearby. Zoe and Enid are lovers. Long shot at dusk in sanddunes. They are covered in sandflies and chat aimlessly of Berlin. Willy initiates a new game, blind man's scrabble. As the game progresses, he slips off blindfold and releases large goannas into tents. The egg-timer is faulty and they play until dawn. Heavy rain and cane toads have cut them off from shops. Food runs out. Lilos punctured by goannas. Craig gets lockjaw and no one can look at him.

He goes on rampage and buries their swimming gear (bathers, snorkels, inflatable banana) while they are abluting/sleeping. Group I Ching under a heavy sky. Intersperse with boxing footage from Seoul?

Budget Notes/Locations: $800 will hardly be enough to get us up north. Alistair C. (Stunts/Goanna Wrangler) has an uncle in Brisbane who did the T-shirts for the Queensland Pavilion at Expo. He will take slides of Straddie, send them down, and we can blow them up and shoot in front of them. Interior tent scenes to be shot at Ray's Tent City, Gardenvale (if Ray can play a retired fisherman).

The Climax: Still no definite idea. Chance meeting with Terence Lewis in a secret nightclub/casino? Don't know. Tomorrow we film hydrofoil sequence at the Marina. Bought textas this morning but maybe it's too late. Tofu poisoning is rampant and most of the crew cannot leave their beds.

WHERE AND WHEN:
'On Shifting Sandshoes' by Paul Davies, 14 Acland Street, St Kilda. Opens November 19; Mondays to Saturdays at 8.30 pm, bookings Bass 11 500 or Theatreworks 534 8986.

The Age, Friday 11 November 1988

THEATRE BEAT

ON SHIFTING SANDSHOES
THEATREWORKS

The novel element of this play first strikes you when you are handed a brightly coloured sun visor and informed that this is the program (keeping with the spirit of things nearly everyone in the audience wore one). The program informs you of the great ideas and symbolism behind the play, which unfortunately sounds much better in the program than they appear transformed on the stage.

Theatreworks have one of the best performing spaces I've seen, particularly suited to this play. It is huge and roomy with very high ceilings and are easily arranged seating plan (shame those plastic seats are so uncomfortable).

The set of this play — a couple of tents, humpy lounge, camp fire and camping paraphernalia added to the atmosphere of summer at the beach and the bright lighting was the exact colour of the summer sun — causing a few in the audience to reach for their sunglasses. The floor was painted with beachy creatures, including a beautiful big starfish that glowed blue in the fluorescent light. There were also simple images projected on the black screens — a smiling sun, blue water, waves and the like.

So the scene is set for the annual gathering of diverse friends who meet to celebrate the tradition of Christmas and New Year with their own traditional habits on Stradbroke Island. Apparently this year things don't run as smoothly as the group used to — it exists for days, their supplies run out, relationships are tested — personalities stripped to the bone and put to the test.

Although the acting was good the characters were stereotypes and therefore predictable. There was your typical male chauvinist beer swilling ocker male, your health freak, your sweetly middle aged gay male, your sweet still trendy thing and her daggy "sensitive" boyfriend, and the typical Aussie tough bitch — coarse flamboyant with an 'I couldn't care less' attitude. They never had anything particularly interesting to say to do. It was like being a fly on the wall in the wrong house.

AMANDA CLARK

ENTERTAINMENT
Top presentation of old theme

By MARK VADAS

"ON Shifting Sandshoes" is a fine and lighthearted piece of Australian theatre by Paul Davies.

The play pitches six characters together on Stradbroke Island for an annual Christmas-New Year camping trip.

Paula, played by Rosie Tonkin, is both flighty and endearing while being encompassed by her lilly-livered boyfriend, Sandy (Brian Nankervis).

The macho figure of Bruce (Ross Williams) is the city developer who eventually is caught out in more than one area of his life.

His wife, Margot, is played by Christine Keogh, better known as the red-haired typist from the hugely successful "Comedy Company" series.

Diane (Jean Kittson) is a tough, fit feminist, one who knows what really is happening behind the scenes.

The final member of this varied party is Raoul, the owner of a struggling vegetarian restaurant. He is wild, enthusiastic and egotistical to the point of nausea. David Swann gives a convincing performance, is thorough, hilarious and delightful.

"ON SHIFTING Sandshoes" by Paul D... vies at Theatreworks cast from le... bottom row: Rosie Tonkin (Paula), Ro... Williams (Bruce), Christine Keogh (Ma... got), David Swann (Raoul), Jean Kittso... (Diane) and Brian Nankervis (Sandy). P... ture by RUTH MADDISON.

THE ARTS

Taking the high ground

Theatre/Jennifer Ellison

With holiday time looming, Theatreworks' *On Shifting Sandshoes* (Acland Street, Melbourne) is a preview of what lies ahead for many people: the annual camping holiday. Paul Davies' comedy captures the sense of ritual which accompanies these pilgrimages and the tensions which inevitably arise among a group of people living in close quarters and trying to have fun. Replete with all the paraphernalia of tents, Eskies, beach balls and zinc cream, Davies' hapless group of six gathers together on Stradbroke Island. Of course, Raoul (David Swann) has forgotten to bring the meat. Sandy (Brian Nankervis) is allergic to anything and everything and Diane (Jean Kittson) cuts a foot on the shovel. Then it rains.

Part of the glee with which audiences can watch this show is that it's them, not us, having to suffer through this abominably awful experience. Davies and the cast obviously had a lot of fun putting the show together and Mark Shirref's direction keeps the pace under control, at least in the first act. When the rain comes and they are literally stranded, the characters start to go troppo and the whole shebang goes over the top.

The characters are intentionally stereotypes, a couple of them rather tacky ones, but Davies has a certain affection for them. The humor is largely wholesome, rather than sour. *On Shifting Sandshoes* is a jolly romp. Anyone who has been on a camping holiday will relate to at least some of these ridiculous experiences. ■

Courier-Mail

BRISBANE, Wednesday, December 28, 1988

Straddie setting for play

THIS week thousands of Australians will dust off their tents, find the gas lamp and head off on a camping trip.

This annual ritual, which can become a comedy of errors, is the basis for the latest hit comedy by Brisbane playwright, Paul Davies.

On Shifting Sandshoes is set on Stradbroke Island during the Christmas/New Year break. A group of friends, four from Brisbane and two from Melbourne, meet for the seventh year at the same camp site.

The rain comes, grudges are aired, food supplies run out and the campers eventually stumble off Stradbroke, unlikely to attempt a return visit.

The play, written as a Bicentennial project, has enjoyed excellent reviews from the hard-to-impress Melbourne drama critics and is likely to be seen in Brisbane in the New Year.

Davies, who now lives in

From LEISA SCOTT in MELBOURNE

Melbourne and writes for the St Kilda-based drama company, TheatreWorks, wrote *On Shifting Sandshoes* from first-hand experience.

"Anybody who has been camping has a disaster story; writing the script was a question of bringing a lot of disaster stories together and making good fun," Davies said.

"The idea of going to the beach with the tent and sleeping under the stars, closing the door on civilisation, is the sort of a urge that is in a lot of Australians."

Davies first became interested in drama when studying for an arts degree at Queensland University. He found that taking part in student revues was more fun than studying.

After a stint at James Cook University teaching English, Davies was offered a scriptwriting job with Crawford Productions. He wrote the last episodes of *Homicide* and the first of *The Sullivans*.

For the past five years, he has been TheatreWorks' playwright and the creator of some of Melbourne's more innovative theatre.

His *Storming St Kilda by Tram* brought theatre to the streets with actors performing on a travelling tram and acting out the weird and often hilarious incidents which any Melbourne commuter has experienced.

Davies tries to visit Brisbane at least twice a year. He hopes one day to write in Brisbane for six months and produce plays in Melbourne for the other six.

Davies looks forward to *On Shifing Sandshoes* playing in Brisbane so that Queenslanders can see a play about themselves from a Victorian point of view.

It would also make casting a little easier. "We had a bit of trouble finding Melbourne actors with suntans to play Queenslanders," Davies joked.

The Emerald Hill, Sandridge and St Kilda Times

Circulating throughout the cities of Port Melbourne, South Melbourne and St Kilda

3 August, 1989 — 79 Bay Street, Port Melbourne 3207. Phone: (03) 646 5040 — Vol. 12 No. 29

Storming on to critical success

By GREG LANGLEY

ST KILDA playwright Paul Davies has gained a bit of a reputation for storming various places.

His play, *Storming St Kilda By Tram*, has stormed its way to critical and tram stop success (and not a little notoriety with the police) and Paul himself last weekend stormed the Australian Writers' Guild Awards in Sydney.

Paul Davies was awarded two 'AWGIES', one for the Best Stage Play in 1988 (*On Shifting Sandshoes*) and one for the Best Play in Community Theatre (*Storming St Kilda By Tram*).

Receiving the awards, he made it clear that he considered the double header a reflection of the ability of the whole Theatreworks company who contributed to the creation of the plays.

"The awards belong as much to the cast and the director, Mark Shirrefs, as they do to me," he told EHT this week.

Paul, originally from Queensland, shifted to Melbourne in 1974 to be the last script writer on *Homocide* and the first on *The Sullivans*.

Apart from his two award winning plays, he has written *Breaking Up In Balwyn* and *Full House/No Vacancies* and his television writing credits include *Against the Wind* and *Rafferty's Rules*.

They're both laughing. Award-winning playwright Paul Davies outside Luna Park.

He says both award winning comedies were triggered by real events. In the case of *Storming St Kilda By Tram*, Paul Davies said he was inspired by an incident between a conductor, a punk and an old drunk which he and Carolyn Howard observed while passengers on a tram in Kew Junction.

"Everyone in Melbourne has a story about trams", he said.

"Trams are places where drama happens all the time and it's a matter of arranging the events and staging them.

"A connie I know who saw the play said she had been through everyone of the events portrayed, though not necessarily in one night."

The Theatreworks company has pioneered a location theatre tradition and, apart from trams, the company has staged plays on riverboats and in Linden Gallery while other Melbourne groups have performed works in court rooms, hotels and police auditoriums.

Paul Davies said Melbourne was far ahead of other Australian capital cities which had no tradition of experimenting with live theatre in this form.

"I think we've proven that you can have experimental theatre and that it can be successful," he said.

"These works have opened up new territory and, hopefully for theatre, exploited that three dimensional aspect which is unique to live theatre and which films and television can never hope to compete with."

He said the potential for places for plays to be performed were only limited by imagination, council fire regulations and possible methods to obtain the money from the audience.

To prove his point, he is currently working on an idea for a performance of *South Pacific* in the St Kilda baths.

"It will be about the exploitation of St Kilda iconography, if I can use that word. Luna Park and Acland Street have become fairly standard backdrops for rock clips and I will be working with this.

"A film crew will come to St Kilda to shoot a cooler advertisement and the audience will be the extras."

He hopes to have the work ready for the comedy festival next year and said it will be a "strictly BYO togs affair."

The Herald, Melbourne, Monday November 21, 1988

Camping carry on is a comedy success

THEATRE

On Shifting Sandshoes
Written by Paul Davies. Directed by Mark Shirrefs. With Jean Kitson, Brian Nankervis, David Swann, Rosie Tonkin and Christine Keogh. A Theatreworks presentation Mon-Sat 8.30 pm; tickets $14.90 ($10.90 conc) special concession night Tuesday $7, group concessions and dinner and show package deals available. At Theatreworks, 14 Acland St, St Kilda. Bookings 534-8986 or Bass
Reviewed by Stephen Radic

THE place: Stradbroke Island. The time: the present. It's Christmas and as they have done for seven years, a group of friends, three men and three women land on the island in search of rest, recreation and a holiday away from the confines of business and city life.

They are a mixed group of individuals whose professions range from land developer to Carlton bookshop owner, hairdresser to restaurateur. Old friends, they have now moved on in life and though they see each other regularly, the basis of their friendship has eroded away into mere habit.

They don't know this, however; it takes one particular weekend away for them to find out the truth about themselves. *On Shifting Sandshoes* is a comedy with several thematic levels to it. It is in part about rituals and pecking orders, while exploring the way in which stress can rip away the superficial veil of civility.

When things go wrong — as they too often do on camping trips — the stress begins to corrode each person's character.

One way to cope with the situation is through games and these the group play endlessly, particularly a species of volleyball dubbed "bastard ball".

As the nasally health fanatic with relationship problems, Jean Kitson brings a grumpy bonhomie to her part.

As gay restaurateur Raoul, David Swann seems to enjoy his part to the point of overshadowing the rest of the cast, that is if Ross Williams' belligerent Bruce will let him or anyone get a word in.

From cut feet and wounded egos to fights over a packet of potato crisps, *On Shifting Sandshoes* is largely successful where humor is concerned, even if an audience won't come away from the show greatly enlightened about the fickleness of human affections.

The Herald Monday Magazine

Look back in laughter

STEPHEN RADIC discovers why Jean Kittson has put her sandshoes on

ANYONE who saw *Let the Blood Run Free* and its two sequels will be familiar with the work of comedienne Jean Kittson.

She played Nurse Pam in that show, "a nice and innocent girl who ends up a Sigourney Weaver-like character" as Kittson herself says.

Since the success of the three soap opera sendups *Let the Blood Run Free*, parts 1 and 2, and *Blood Capsule*, Kittson has hardly looked back.

"Because those shows were so successful," she says, "there was a lot of exposure and lots of work. That was 1984 — I haven't been out of work since."

Her career has been a mixed basket of comedy and straight acting roles, ranging from teaching drama in the Mallee region for a year, to working in Sydney with a theatre-in-education company called Tow Truck. Several years in Sydney were followed by a trip overseas, then a return to Melbourne.

"I'd never worked professionally in Melbourne and I thought how am I going to get work? La Joke at Le Joke were having tryouts so I went along. If you can do comedy, it's much easier to get work. You can do a gig and pay the gas bill whereas with theatre you have to wait for a company to employ you."

From Le Joke, Kittson gained a part in *Snakepit*, at the Church Theatre, and a little later was to appear as innocent Nurse Pam at the Last Laugh Theatre Restaurant.

Three sellout shows later, Kittson was back at La Joke at Le Joke, doing *Bedlam*, a one-person monologue, explicit and occasionally controversial, on the subject of "being in bed", where appropriately enough the performance took place in a double bed.

"The first five nights were fine, she remembers, "then on the Saturday night a table of young drunks turned the thing into a disaster.

"The trouble is when you have a structured monologue, the rhythms are important and to break them breaks the whole flow. Of course, you have certain comebacks up your sleeve. You have to find some way of coming back

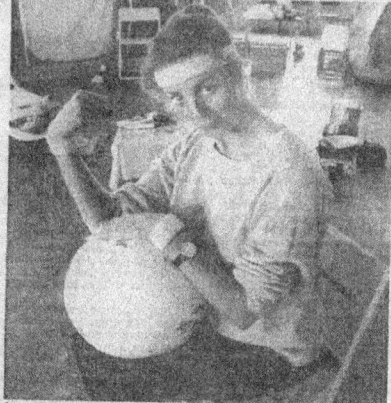

Jean Kittson ... taking on the role of a sports fanatic.

but often the audience loves the comebacks more than the material. It's their chance to be funny, you see."

1988 has seen Kittson in a variety of quite divergent stage roles. In Gary Hutchinson's *Angela* at the Court House Theatre, she played the part of a stripper. She also appeared in the *Fawlty Towers*-style venture *Casa del Tawdry* where the audience stayed overnight in an East Melbourne guesthouse and were subjected to all manner of comic indignities.

Kittson then wrote *Off the Tracks* for the St Martin's Theatre, wrote and performed *Bedlam*, as well as a second

has done part-time publicity work for the Valhalla Cinema and presently she is in rehearsal with *On Shifting Sandshoes*, a comedy by Paul Davies, billed as "surviving the great Australian holiday".

"It's a play about six people who regularly go on Christmas holidays to Stradbroke Island," Kittson explains.

"One of the women, Paula, was a teacher and wants to join a rock and roll women's band and has taken up with Sandy, a Carlton bookshop owner. He is a hypochondriac with phobias, allergies and skin problems.

"The woman who really runs the camp is Margo, married to Bruce, a land developer, a capitalist pig with absolutely no morals.

"I play Diane, a sports fanatic and a teacher who sublimates a lot of her relationship problems by jogging.

"They set up camp, go through the rituals of who's in charge of what and they play their own special game called bastard ball."

But of course nothing goes to plan in this storyline, rain swells the creeks, cutting them off from civilisation, friendships strain and provisions run low.

On Shifting Sandshoes is a Theatreworks production, that company being best known for its travelling theatre piece *Storming Mont Albert By Tram*, *Breaking Up in Balwyn* and the 11-week sellout last August, *After Dinner*.

"*Sandshoes* is really about old friends who are incompatible now," Kittson elaborates, "it's about how they reveal themselves in very trying situations."

■ On Shifting Sandshoes opens at Theatreworks, 14 Acland St, St Kilda on November 16. Bookings: 534-8986 or Bass.

Round up

• PAULA deBURGH •

On Shifting Sandshoes
Theatreworks
November 19 to December 10

THEATREWORKS have done it again! A laugh a minute to the call of the wild, in Paul Davies's camping epic, *On Shifting Sandshoes*.

A group of friends meet each Christmas for a camping holiday on Stradbroke Island. This annual ritual is usually carefree, except on this, the Bicentennial year, when things go awry. Storm clouds gather, the heavens open, and it rains and rains. The group is stranded from the mainland, relationships become strained, personas begin to drop away, as the fight for survival begins.

On Shifting Sandshoes is exceptionally well cast, with superb performances from everyone, under the confident direction of Mark Shirrefs. The stage design and graphics by Amanda Johnson enhance the production.

Paul Davies is developing into a major comic satirist and his plays are always worth seeing. I challenge anyone not to enjoy this latest offering at Theatreworks.

Surviving the Australian holiday

Theatreworks' new Play *On Shifting Sandshoes* opens next week. Writer Paul Davies has based the show on his real life experience of getting stranded on Queensland's Stradbroke Island with a group of people he hung out with in his University youth. The Big Chill hits the warm group as they face the prospect of no food, their mid thirties and heavens to Betsy, no liquid refreshments. Come back to Stradbroke Island Jimmy Dean Jimmy Dean.

Brian Nankervis describes the show as a "black comedy where the six characters examine themselves through a series of games." This Lord of the Flies for people facing mid life crises brings together a licorice all sorts of characters. There's Brian's character, Sandy Mills, a Carlton Bookshop owner who's a bozo intellectual. He's followed by Raoul Mahou, a French Swiss New Caledonian who runs a Mediterranean Restaurant in Brisbane and Dianne Willis, a health obsessed teacher who's fixated by her own body. And I must mention the character of Pauline Casey, a school teacher who's given up the chalkface to sing with an all women band.

I'm looking forward to seeing this Return of the Stradbroke Six. The menagerie of characters promises both a funny and thoughtful night.

GAGLINES - by Derek Holmes.

Melbourne Review / Melbourne Times

Theatre 1988: the signs have been healthy

By CHRIS BOYD

In spite of the fact that 1988 has been a year of upheaval, the theatre scene in Melbourne has rarely been healthier. More than 50 new Australian plays appeared during the year. Most were worth seeing and several were first class. More than 40 were produced by fringe companies. In spite of this avalanche of theatre, attendances have, on the whole, been good.

La Mama, now almost 22 years old, is still the most fertile source of quality Australian plays. This year it christened plays of great calibre by Andrew Bovell, Barry Dickens, Steve J Spears, Frank Bren, and Alex Buzo. Each of those plays was superbly staged.

Theatreworks, too, have had a good year. They stumbled on a couple of winners, *Storming St Kilda by Tram* and *On Shifting Sandshoes*, and picked up the successful La Mama's production of Bovell's *After Dinner*.

Australian Nouveau Theatre had a lacklustre year after the great Chekhov trilogy of 1987. Apart from the revival of Jean-Pierre Mignon's production of *Summer of the Seventeenth Doll* there was little of note. Their Spoleto production of *Molière* was particularly disappointing.

It has been quiet, too, in Hawthorn. Just days ago, the Contemporary Theatre Company, which operates from The Church Theatre, was bailed out of its financial difficulties — albeit temporarily. *Volpone*, directed by The Magus Robert Draffin, was the highlight of their year.

"Draft" was also responsible for *Ship of Fools* by Andrew Bovell and *Whistling in the Theatre*. His imagination and sheer theatricality make him my choice for best director of 1988.

The Flash Rat company seemed to crawl out of nowhere! Their three productions were entertaining and well executed. Nancy Black's performance in *Second Lady - USA* was outstanding. The Roundhouse company, though, gets my gong as the best newcomer of 1988 for their verve, drill and sheer energy.

Melbourne Writer's Theatre, in Carlton, turned out a handful of well crafted plays but seemed unwilling to spend money on advertising!

On the mainstream front, both major companies have new artistic directors. Carrillo Gantner recently seized the reins in a bloodless coup at Playbox. The previous artistic director, Peter Oyston, presided over a fairly dismal year. In 1988 Playbox presented two of the worst Australian plays I have seen in many years.

Having said that, Playbox deserves credit for picking up Sarah Cathcart's brilliant one woman show *The Serpents Fall*, and for joining with the Next Wave festival in producing *Riff-Raff - The Remix*.

The "odd couple" of Melbourne Theatre, Roger Hodgman and Simon Phillips, have been running the MTC all year. The Melbourne Theatre Company has had an excellent year. It has shaken off its reputation for mediocrity.

Superb productions were mounted of *Les Liaisons Dangereuses*, *The First Born Trilogy* by Jack Davis, and *As You Like It*. Two of the best, *Serious Money* and *The Rivers of China*, were directed by Simon Phillips. He is living proof that you can teach an old dog new tricks. He has dragged the company out of its conservative slumber and given it a damn good shake.

Sensibly, from a financial point of view at least, the MTC mounted two co-productions with the Sydney Theatre Company. Surprisingly perhaps, given the enormous difference in taste and temperament between capital city audiences, both plays fared remarkably well.

Dinkum Assorted was good, clean fun without drodging the lowest common denominator, while Caryl Churchill's *Serious Money* stretched the boundaries of drama by presenting a financial murder mystery in rhyming verse.

Playbox is feeling the squeeze. Their niche in the market has been severely eroded by a taut and vibrant MTC on one side, and by the increasing quality and professionalism of the fringe companies on the other.

Playbox appears to "turn the tide", or at least halt the erosion, in 1989, by moving four of their seven plays in Season 1 to Anthill in South Melbourne. Anthill seats 100, and should be far more cost effective (and look a lot less empty than the Studio.

Two of the theatre companies which had success in 1988 were Theatreworks in St Kilda and the Melbourne Theatre Company. Top: The team of Theatreworks "misfits" who are still drawing crowds to On Shifting Sandshoes.

more primitive, sinister, inner urban sleaze of all-night bars and a certain streetwise desperation.

In his research for 'LIVING ROOMS', Paul discovered an interesting fact – the St. Kilda rail line was the oldest regular passenger line in Australia. When this line was threatened with closure in late 1986, diverse community groups banded together to campaign against the move. This play was a way of focusing the issue.

Already audiences at Theatreworks are enjoying Paul's very funny, latest play, 'ON SHIFTING SANDSHOES', directed by Mark Shirrefs who also directed 'STORMING ST. KILDA BY TRAM'. The play is about a diverse group of friends who go camping together every Christmas/New Year on Stradbroke Island, in Queensland. However, this Bicentennial year, things go riotously out of kilter.

Says Paul, 'Camping by the beach is a very Australian way. To go to the beach is an Australian habit. It struck me there are a lot of parallels to the way Australia started – Sydney, the tents in a foreign land, diminishing food, eskys and such. So we are stranding these people in the play, putting them under pressure for survival. What starts out as a joyous camping 'get-together' turns very sour. You can see the parallels between how Australia started and this annual traditional camping holiday.'

In this play, the vigorous games of bastard ball and frisbee are replaced with the dividing of the last sardines and spelling out SOS with the tinnies.

'I have always been interested in this,' continues Paul. 'As a kid I remember people from the same street, town or work, would all go camping together. They would spend the holidays sitting on the beach, drinking, eating, talking. They would indulge themselves, thinking this is the ultimate.

'If there's anything worth celebrating to finish this special year, it's things like the annual Christmas camp.'

I'm sure the residents of Melbourne would agree as they migrate to the water's edge for a great summer's break. Make sure you get to Theatreworks, though, and pick up a few tips on surviving the perennial Australian holiday.

For bookings contact: Theatreworks, Tel: 534 8986 or 534 4879.

THE MELBURNIAN
The Magazine of the green heart of Australia.
Vol. 2 N.5 Dec–Jan $3.95

The cast of 'On Shifting Sandshoes' rehearse on St Kilda beach.

Theatreworks has done it again

THEATREWORKS has another hit on its hands. The St Kilda based drama company, renowned for such outrageous ventures as 'Storming Mont Albert by Tram' (set on a moving Number 42 tram), 'Breaking up in Balwyn' (set on a boat on the Yarra) and 'Storming St Kilda by Tram', has taken the mickey out of the great Australian holiday.

'On Shifting Sandshoes', written by Paul Davies with taut direction by Mark Shirrefs, is a riotous comedy of errors.

Possessing elements of 'The Big Chill', 'Wake in Fright' and 'Lord of the Flies' without the tears, it is set on Stradbroke Island, near Brisbane, where a group of friends take their annual camping Christmas break.

This vacation, however, is plagued with disasters. The food runs out, the weather turns nasty and with it the relationships of the motley collection of recognizable types. The reunion comprises Bruce, a boorish Queensland property developer, his long suffering wife, Margot; Diane, a health conscious high school teacher; Sandy, a sensitive, effeminate bookshop owner; Paula, his timid girlfriend and Raoul, a gay flamboyant restaurateur.

Performances from the talented cast had the audience in hysterics throughout the evening as the characters battled for survival.

AUSTRALIAN VISITORS NEWS

TheatreWorks ON SHIFTING SANDSHOES by Paul Davies

FROM **NOVEMBER 19**
Mon-Sat 8.30 pm
AT THEATREWORKS
14 Acland Street, St. Kilda
Bookings:
BASS 11500 or
THEATREWORKS 534 8986
Excellent group concessions,
dinner & show package!

THE arts

ON SHIFTING SANDSHOES
By Paul Davies

THE latest from Theatreworks, the company that earlier this year brought you the comedy hits of the year, Storming St Kilda By Tram and After Dinner!

On Shifting Sandshoes is about a diverse group of friends who go camping together every Christmas/New Year on Stradbroke Island. However, this year, the Bicentennial year, things go riotously out of kilter; it begins to rain nd doesn't let up for days! The creek rises and cuts them off from civilisation ... the holiday now becomes a struggle for survival!

Friendships are strained, belongings are soggy, food becomes scarce. Relationships are stripped to the bone! The vigorous games of 'Bastard Ball' are replaced by the divving up of the last sardine and the spelling out of S.O.S. on the beach in XXXX empties!

The play is about migration within Australia ... the annual Christmas trek. It's about playing games and having fun. It's about relationships that extend beyond family, and about the strain on those bonds when the food runs out! It's a very funny play from the author of Storming St Kilda By Tram and Living Rooms, both huge Theatreworks successes.

On Shifting Sandshoes is directed by Mark Shirrefs, who also directed Storming St Kilda By Tram and Cake, as wellas the earlier Theatreworks hits, Storming Mont Albert By Tram and Breaking Up In Balwyn (both by Paul Davies as well).

On Shifting Sandshoes opens on November 16 for a limited season, Mondays to Saturdays at 8.30 pm at Theatreworks, 14 Acland Street, St Kilda (Enter Acland St at Carlisle St).

Book at BASS 11500, or Theatreworks 534 8986. Tickets $14.90, $10.90. (On Tuesdays concession price is $7.00.)

Excellent concessions available for groups of 20 and over! Also special dinner-and-show package deals for groups. Ring Shirley or Wolfgang 534 8986 or 534 4879.

POSTER 2009

PROGRAMME 2009

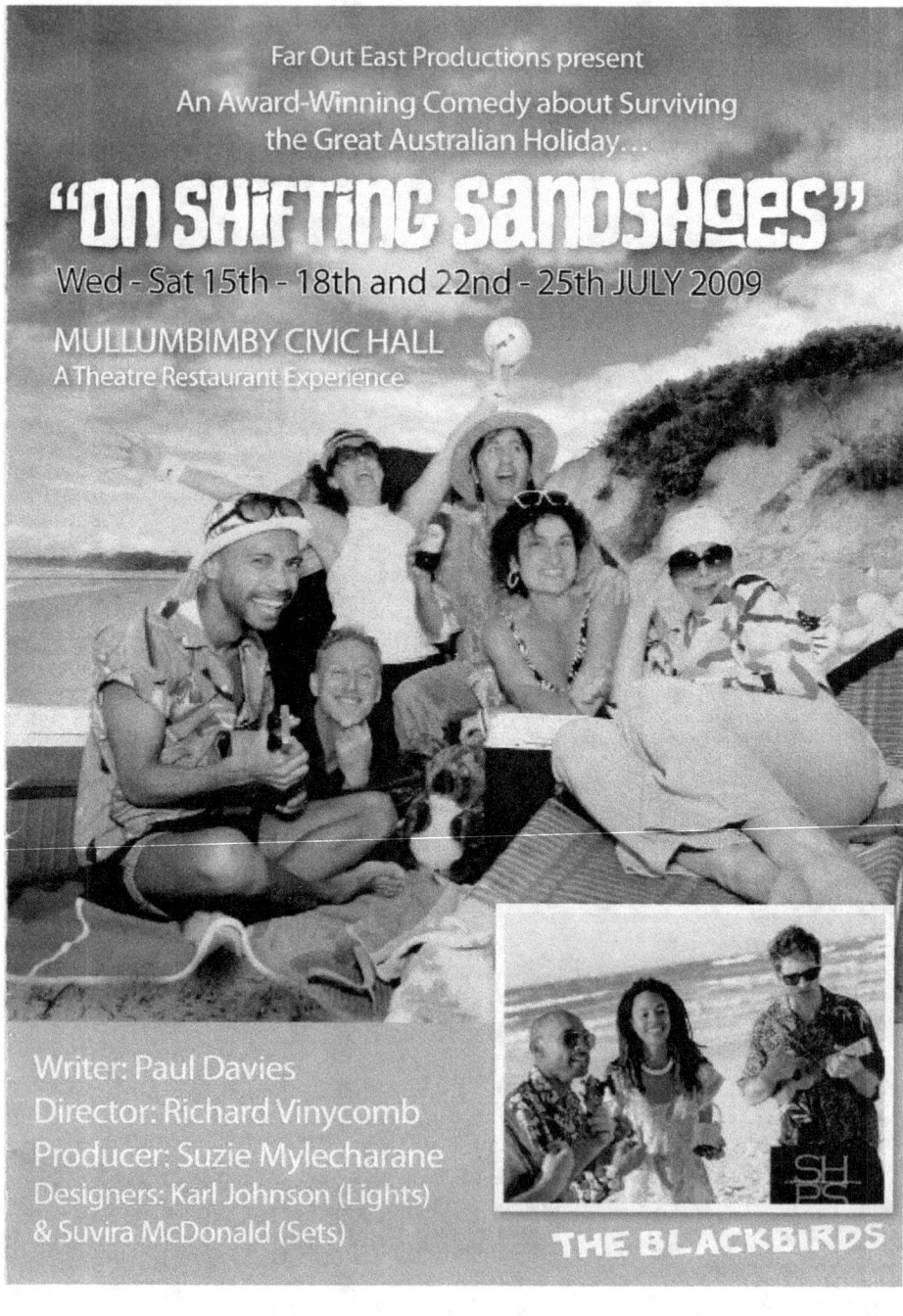

Paul Davies is an award winning screenwriter, script editor and playwright who sharpened his quill on over a hundred episodes of Teledrama from classic Crawford series such as *Homicide* (1974-5), *The Box* (1975-76) *The Sullivans* (1976-78) and *Skyways* (1979), to *Rafferty's Rules* (1985), *Blue Heelers* (1997), *Pacific Drive* (1996), *Stingers* (1998-2003), *Something in the Air* (1999-2001) and *Headland* (2005). He also helped spark the site-specific performance revolution in Melbourne in the 1980s with TheatreWorks' production of his first play *Storming Mont Albert By Tram* (1982). What became known as *The Tram Show* played across a dozen years to packed trams in both Melbourne and Adelaide, travelling a total distance that would have taken the show halfway round the world. Its success lead to an outbreak of 'location theatre' in Melbourne throughout the 1980s including three other plays in real places: *Breaking Up In Balwyn* (1983, on a riverboat), *Living Rooms* (1986, in an historic mansion) and *Full House/No Vacancies* (1989, in a boarding house). These works became the subject of his thesis *Really Moving Drama*.

Both *The Tram Show* and *On Shifting Sandshoes* (1988) were awarded AWGIES, along with *Return of The Prodigal* (2000) an episode of *Something In The Air* (ABC). Paul co-wrote the feature *Neil Lynn* with David Baker in 1984, and the docu-fiction *Exits* (1980) with Pat Laughren and Carolyn Howard. His novel, *33 Postcards From Heaven* was published by Gondwana Press in 2005. Numerous articles, reviews, stories and interviews have been published in *Metro, Cinema Papers, Cantrill's Filmnotes, Australasian Drama Studies, Community Theatre In Australia, The Macquarie Companion to the Australian Media* and *Theatre Research International* (Cambridge University). He co-wrote three documentaries with John Hughes (*All That Is Solid, Traps and One Way Street*) as well as *Holy Rollers* with Rosie Jones. Paul has also given courses in literature and creative writing at various colleges and universities including: Southern Cross, James Cook and Melbourne State.

FOR CAZ HOWARD
1952-1990

www.ingramcontent.com/pod-product-compliance
Lightning Source LLC
Chambersburg PA
CBHW071919290426
44110CB00013B/1410